MY
FAVOURITE
INGREDIENTS

◊

PHOTOGRAPHY BY
Jason Lowe

Quadrille

SKYE GYNGELL

My *favourite*
ingredients

Introduction 6

Asparagus 10

Cherries 26

Fish & Shellfish 40

Olive oil 60

Leaves 70

Citrus 86

Pulses & Grains 106

Tomatoes 120

Nuts 140

Vinegar 158

Garlic 166

Game 178

Apples 194

Cheese 206

Honey 224

Chocolate 234

Index 250

Acknowledgements 255

Please use sea salt, freshly ground pepper and fresh herbs (except in the rare instances where I have specified dried herbs).

I use medium eggs – organic and free-range. Anyone who is pregnant or in a vulnerable health group should avoid recipes using raw egg whites or lightly cooked eggs.

Timings are for fan-assisted ovens. If you are using a conventional oven, turn the setting up by 10–15°C (1/2 Gas mark). Use an oven thermometer to keep a check on the temperature.

Introduction

More than anything else, I would describe my cooking as produce driven. At the restaurant, we compose our menus daily – when the fresh produce arrives and we know for certain what is available and at its best. It is when I see the beautiful cream and crimson fleck of the first Castelfranco of the year, for example, that I begin to consider what it would work with – perhaps succulent fresh crab or the sweet bitter flavour of blood oranges, or maybe young pecorino or oven-roasted pigeon. It might be the particular colour of an olive oil or the sweet intensity of a type of vinegar that gives a certain dish its real character for me. Beautiful ingredients will take a dish to new heights.

At the restaurant we follow the seasons closely. I believe that food eaten in its right season and grown as close to home as possible tastes far better than food flown in from afar. I also believe that nature provides ingredients in the same season that go together perfectly. Pairing seasonal produce is where I have the most fun in the kitchen.

I express myself through the way I cook. Food truly captures my heart, and the kitchen is where I feel confident and at home. Nowhere else do I feel so free, nor so connected at the same time. Food fascinates, seduces and entrances me. Produce in its purest form, in peak condition – tasting as it should – can lift and dazzle me with the excitement of its possibilities.

My knowledge of produce – its history, place, variety and season, as well as learning how to prepare and use it – has come to me gradually over the years and I'm still on a voyage of discovery. I continue, for example, to learn about the varieties and nuances of flavour of all the different honeys. Year in, year out, I come across a different variety of bean, or salad leaf that I fall in love with and wonder how it was possible to cook without it.

Seeking out good produce has introduced me to many local suppliers and farmers over the years – we currently work with no less than 47 different providers. These people are important to me and my relationships with them have developed over time. They are experts on their particular produce and I learn so much from them. I'm fortunate to work in an industry where people are willing to pass on knowledge and information, because they have a genuine desire to share their passion.

As a small child, my mother would tell me that I asked too many questions and I really haven't changed. I am endlessly inquisitive, especially when it comes to food, and have a burning desire to learn everything I can about produce and cooking. Plus, I seem to have an amazing capacity to forget and need to re-learn my craft, which never ceases to amaze me!

As a cook, for me it is important to move forward, to always maintain an inquisitiveness, to try new things. When employing a new young cook in the kitchen, I don't look for speed, knife skills or even organisational ability, although the latter is on some level important. Instead, I am more interested in how they react to the produce as it arrives. Do they look excited and inspired? Do they handle ingredients gently with respect and appreciation? If the answers are yes, then I know we will work well together.

Since writing my first book, *A Year in my Kitchen*, my cooking has evolved in subtle ways that would probably pass unnoticed to anyone else. It has become simpler, more produce inspired. Flavours are now more inclined to whisper than roar. Dishes are very definitely layered still, but those layers are lighter, cleaner and perhaps more ethereal. As I have grown in confidence, I find myself paring down my cooking, interfering less if you like. My intention is to make the produce taste even more of itself and the season to which it belongs.

More than ever I welcome in the new season's produce, which arrives almost on a weekly basis through the year. It makes me excited and smile when the first peach of the year perfectly ripens in one of our greenhouses, or winter purslane makes an appearance after nine months of absence. Tomatoes are greeted with great cheer in midsummer, yet come late autumn I'm ready to pick cavolo nero after the first frost of the year. There is no better way of understanding what each season has to offer than to have a vegetable garden, however small.

My Favourite Ingredients highlights some of the rich and beautiful ingredients that I am privileged to work with through the culinary year. Most of the recipes are simple in their execution. For certain, there are no daunting or complicated techniques... just simple ways of combining good produce in order to maximise and fully appreciate its flavours. In keeping with my reverence for the seasons, starring ingredients are married with ingredients that are around at the same time, for nature cleverly provides perfectly balanced partners.

Many of the dishes are part of our repertoire at the restaurant. Pulses and grains, nuts, game, fish and shellfish, and seasonal fruits and vegetables feature strongly in our dishes, along with abundant fresh herbs and beautiful olive oils. This type of cooking requires a warm-hearted approach and attention to the senses, but most importantly of all, it calls for an awe-inspiring reverence of the bounty this earth creates. Enjoy...

Cooking is
not about being
the best or most
perfect cook, but rather
it is about sharing the
table with family and
friends.

Asparagus

I am always eager for the first box of English asparagus to arrive. The season traditionally straddles May and early June, and lasts just six weeks in total, but it can vary a little. Young asparagus spears are the tender shoots of a much larger plant, which if left alone will grow over a metre tall, with fern-like fronds and brilliant vermillion-coloured berries. As the spears start poking their fine heads above the ground in early spring, they are generally harvested when bright green and no more than 20–25cm high.

White asparagus is, in fact, the same plant, whose shoots have been banked by earth as they grow, keeping the spears underground and preventing them from turning green. In this way, the asparagus is blanched and the spears grow plump, smooth and white except for their tips, which are tinged violet.

Asparagus is generally graded by size and sold in bunches. Size varies from stalks that are no thicker than fine pencils to ones that are as large and fat as Havana cigars.

Like most vegetables, asparagus starts to lose its sweetness as soon as it is picked from the ground, so it is important to choose the freshest possible specimens. Spears should be firm, smooth and brightly coloured with a vibrant bloom to the stem. Look for heads that are tightly formed and compact. All too often asparagus is picked after it has bolted. If this is the case, the buds will have begun to open and spread apart and the tiny branches under the heads will have opened up. Avoid asparagus like this, as it will usually be tougher and possibly taste a little bitter. Also check that the cut ends are not dry and white, indicating that they have not been freshly cut.

Use asparagus as soon as possible after buying. If you need to store it briefly, treat it like cut flowers – stand the spears upright in a jar of water and place in the fridge.

◊

To prepare asparagus for cooking, grasp each spear between both hands and snap it. It will break at the woody end – just above where the stalk will be tender. You can save the woody ends for flavouring soup. I like to peel the lower part of the stalks if they are anything other than very slender. The skin on larger asparagus, in particular, tends to be tougher and slightly fibrous. Asparagus is easy to peel using a swivel vegetable peeler; it takes seconds and is well worth the effort.

◊

To boil asparagus, simply plunge into well-salted boiling water and cook until just tender when pierced with a knife. Cooking time will depend largely on the size and thickness of the spears, but as a general rule of thumb, it should take about 1¹/₂ minutes, and no longer than 3 minutes. When cooked, asparagus should take on an intense green colour. White asparagus, which is much thicker, can take up to 8 minutes to cook through. Once cooked, serve at once or cool quickly, by draining and spreading the spears out on a board, so that they retain their lovely, appealing colour. Asparagus is also delicious simply brushed with oil, seasoned and grilled over a barbecue or grill; it takes no longer than a few minutes.

We don't grow asparagus in our vegetable garden, mainly because it takes up a lot of space to produce a small harvest – almost a metre per plant. Also, grown from seed it takes 4–5 years to produce the first spears – a real test of patience. Nevertheless, we buy English green and French white asparagus in season, using both varieties in as many ways as we possibly can, firstly because they are delicious, and secondly because they signal so loudly the arrival of spring.

Now I associate asparagus with gentle warmth and dappled skies, but one of my abiding childhood memories is of eating tinned asparagus on sweltering Christmas days in Australia. It was always cold from the fridge and so soggy that it would disintegrate in the mouth, yet strangely I enjoyed the flavour at the time...

Asparagus with Tabasco butter

I make a lot of flavoured butters – they are a really good way to enhance simply grilled meat, fish and vegetables. The possible flavourings are endless, from the famous café de Paris butter that has just about everything in it, to this very simple butter. We most often serve it with cracked crab claws, but in spring we sometimes use it for this simple starter.

Serves 4

about 32 green asparagus spears

sea salt and freshly ground black pepper

Tabasco butter

200g unsalted butter, at room temperature

1 heaped tbsp Dijon mustard

25 drops of Tabasco

juice of 1/2 lemon

First make the flavoured butter. Place the butter in a blender along with the mustard, Tabasco, lemon juice and a good pinch of salt. Whiz until all the ingredients are well combined. Remove from the blender and spoon the butter into a small bowl. Cover and place in the fridge. Return to room temperature when ready to use. (This butter can be made a day or so in advance.)

To cook the asparagus, bring a large pot of well-salted water to the boil. Snap the woody ends off the asparagus, and peel the bottom 5cm or so of the stalks, using a swivel vegetable peeler. When the water is boiling vigorously, drop in the asparagus and cook for 1 1/2 minutes or until it is just tender to the bite.

Drain the asparagus in a colander and place in a warm bowl. Add half the flavoured butter and toss through the asparagus, then season with a little pepper.

Divide among warm plates and dot each pile of asparagus with a knob of the remaining butter. Serve while still piping hot.

Perfectly cooked green asparagus has a majestic flavour and texture, but if over-cooked, it can be very disappointing. Don't leave the pan unattended during cooking – asparagus takes very little time to become tender, while retaining a bite, which is what you are aiming for.

Asparagus with tomato dressing and crème fraîche

This a lovely asparagus starter. The tomato dressing has an intensity that contrasts well with the slightly nutty flavour of briefly cooked asparagus – and soft, gentle crème fraîche bridges the gap between the two flavours beautifully.

Serves 4

about 32 asparagus spears

sea salt and freshly ground black pepper

1 tbsp extra virgin olive oil

4 tbsp crème fraîche

Tomato dressing

12 little ripe tomatoes

200ml extra virgin olive oil, plus extra to drizzle

2 rosemary sprigs, leaves only

1 garlic clove, peeled

4 good-quality tinned anchovy fillets in olive oil, drained

1 tbsp Dijon mustard

1 tbsp good-quality red wine vinegar

To finish

rosemary sprigs with flowers or finely chopped parsley

First make the tomato dressing. Preheat the oven to 200°C/Gas 6. Pierce each tomato once with a small sharp knife – this helps to release the juice while the tomatoes are cooking. Place them in a roasting tin in which they fit quite snugly. Drizzle over a little olive oil and season with salt and pepper. Roast on the middle shelf of the oven for 20 minutes or until the tomatoes are soft and bursting from their skins. Set aside to cool.

Pound the rosemary leaves, garlic and anchovy fillets to a rough paste, using a pestle and mortar. Add the tomatoes one by one, pounding after each addition, until all have been incorporated. Add the mustard and wine vinegar and stir well to combine. Pour in the olive oil, stirring as you do so. Taste and season with a little salt and pepper. The dressing should be quite coarse and textural. Set aside to allow the flavours to adjust to each other.

To cook the asparagus, place a large pan of well-salted water on to boil. Snap the asparagus spears near the base – they will naturally break off where the fibrous part ends. Peel the lower end of the stalks. When the water is boiling vigorously, drop in the asparagus and cook for 1½ minutes or until the spears are still firm but yield to the bite. Remove with tongs and place in a warm bowl.

Immediately season the asparagus and dress with the extra virgin olive oil. Arrange on warm plates, add a dollop of crème fraîche and spoon on the tomato dressing. Finish with rosemary flowers, if available, or sprinkle with a little chopped parsley and serve.

Asparagus, rice and pancetta soup

Rather more of a really wet sloppy risotto than a soup, this is one of my all-time favourite recipes. It is rich and robust, with its roots definitely earthbound. Very, very satisfying ...

Serves 4

50ml extra virgin olive oil, plus extra to serve

2 red onions, peeled and finely chopped

small bunch of thyme, leaves only

sea salt and freshly ground black pepper

5 slices of pancetta, chopped into small pieces

3 garlic cloves, peeled and crushed

100g white rice

1 litre good chicken stock

500ml water

12 green asparagus spears

100g Parmesan, freshly grated

2 tbsp chopped parsley

Warm the olive oil in a heavy-based saucepan large enough to hold all the ingredients comfortably. Add the onions, thyme and a pinch of salt and sweat over a gentle heat for 10 minutes until the onions are soft, sweet and translucent.

Add the pancetta pieces with the garlic and cook for a further 5–10 minutes, then add the rice and stir well. Immediately pour in the stock and water, and bring to a simmer. Turn down the heat to fairly low, cover the pan and cook until the rice is nutty to the bite; this will take about 20 minutes.

While the rice is cooking, prepare the asparagus. Snap off and discard the woody ends, peel the lower part of the stems, then slice the stalks on the diagonal into short lengths. Add the asparagus to the soup and cook for 2–3 minutes until it is just tender. Add the Parmesan and stir. Season to taste with plenty of black pepper and a good pinch of salt.

Ladle the soup into warm soup plates, sprinkle with the parsley and drizzle with a generous spoonful of extra virgin olive oil.

In the kitchen I talk a lot about using the right-sized pots and pans. An overcrowded pan really doesn't make for good food in my opinion. I like heavy-based pans that are wide at the base with sides that are relatively low. I find it hard to make a connection with the food I am cooking if I have to peer too deeply into a saucepan!

Asparagus with ginger and garlic

Served simply with some plain steamed white rice, this is perfect for a light lunch or supper. In the springtime I often make this dish when I get home from work, tired but not necessarily very hungry. I find it a light, clean, stimulating supper. It is also very good as an accompaniment to white fish.

Serves 4

12–16 green asparagus spears

2–3cm piece of fresh root ginger

1 tbsp sunflower oil

1 garlic clove, peeled and finely sliced

1 red chilli, deseeded and finely sliced

80ml water

1½ tbsp oyster sauce, or to taste

freshly ground black pepper

Snap the woody ends off the asparagus and peel the lower end of the stalks, then cut the spears on the diagonal into 4cm lengths. Peel the ginger and slice into fine rounds, then into the finest possible matchsticks.

Place a wok over a medium-low heat and add the sunflower oil. When it is warm, add the ginger and cook for a few moments to release the flavour.

Add the asparagus, garlic and chilli, and toss to mix, then pour in the water and turn the heat to high. Cook for a minute, then add the oyster sauce. Toss well to coat the asparagus and cook for a further 30 seconds or so until it is tender but retains a bite.

Remove from the heat and taste for seasoning. It shouldn't need any salt as the oyster sauce will give it all the saltiness it needs, but you might like to add a grinding of pepper. Serve very hot.

Asparagus with agretti, chilli oil and poached skate

Agretti is a tangy marsh grass, which – like asparagus – is in season during the spring and the two are natural partners. If you can't find agretti, then use young spinach instead, blanching it for a few seconds only until barely wilted. Delicate poached skate is wonderful served at room temperature with these vibrant vegetables. A drizzle of chilli oil adds a touch of warmth to the finished dish.

Serves 4

400g skate wings

mild-tasting extra virgin olive oil, to drizzle

sea salt and freshly ground black pepper

lemon juice, to taste

12 asparagus spears

bunch of agretti

Poaching liquor

2 carrots, peeled and chopped

1 leek, trimmed, washed and chopped

2 celery sticks, chopped

2 bay leaves

4 parsley sprigs

a few thyme sprigs

5 black peppercorns

Chilli oil

1 red pepper

4 red chillies

juice of 1/2 lemon

300ml mild-tasting extra virgin olive oil

To serve

lemon wedges

For the poaching liquor, put a pan of water on to boil (one that is large enough to hold all the ingredients). Add the carrots, leek and celery, along with the herbs and peppercorns. Once the water has returned to the boil, carefully add the skate wings and immediately turn off the heat. Allow the fish to cook in the residual heat of the poaching liquor as it cools.

When the fish is warm (no longer too hot to handle), carefully remove it using a slotted spoon and place in a bowl. Using your fingers, slide the flesh from its fan-like cartilage framework and break into shreds with your fingers. Place in a bowl and dress with a little extra virgin olive oil. Season lightly with salt and pepper and finish with a few drops of lemon juice. Set aside while you make the chilli oil.

Preheat the grill to high and grill the red pepper until the skin is charred and blistered all over, turning as necessary. Now place in a bowl, cover tightly with cling film and set aside; the steam will help to lift the skin. Do the same with the chillies, which will blacken much more quickly. When cool, peel off the skin from the pepper and chillies – it should come away easily. Slice in half and scrape out the core and seeds.

Pound the pepper and chillies with a good pinch of salt to a rough paste, using a pestle and mortar. Add the lemon juice and pour in the olive oil, stirring well to combine. You should have a vibrant, orangey-red, sludgy thick sauce. Set aside while you cook the asparagus and agretti.

Snap the ends off the asparagus and peel the lower end of the stalks. Put a large pot of well-salted water on to boil. Wash the agretti in several changes of cold water and pick over, chopping off the pink woody ends and removing any less than perfect fronds. When the water is boiling, plunge in the agretti and cook for a minute, then remove with a slotted spoon to a bowl. Dress while still warm with a little extra virgin olive oil. Now cook the asparagus in the same water for 2 minutes. Drain and dress also with a little oil.

To assemble, put the agretti and asparagus into a bowl, add the poached skate and toss very gently to combine. Season with a little salt and pepper and add a few drops of lemon juice. Arrange on individual plates and lightly spoon over the chilli oil. Serve with lemon wedges for squeezing.

Gratin of white asparagus

This rich, creamy gratin of beautiful white asparagus wrapped in a cosy blanket is delicious paired with a simple roast chicken. A leafy green salad – tossed with a dressing that has a note of acidity – is the only other accompaniment you need. Alternatively, you can serve this gratin as it is, with some warm bread to mop up the sauce and, perhaps, some finely sliced porcini mushrooms on the side, dressed with no more than beautiful olive oil, sea salt and black pepper.

Serves 4

60g unsalted butter, melted

15 white asparagus

small bunch of lemon thyme, leaves only

200ml crème fraîche

1 tbsp Dijon mustard

sea salt and freshly ground black pepper

1 cup (60g) fresh white breadcrumbs

80g Parmesan, freshly grated

2 tbsp finely chopped curly parsley

Preheat the oven to 220°C/Gas 7. Brush a copper or ceramic gratin dish with a little of the melted butter.

Trim the asparagus: you will find that white asparagus needs to be trimmed much higher – roughly halfway up the stalks, as a rule of thumb. Slice the spears in half lengthways and lay them in the buttered gratin dish. Sprinkle with most of the lemon thyme leaves, saving a few for garnish.

Now put the crème fraîche and mustard into a heavy-based saucepan and place over a medium heat. Stir to combine and bring to a simmer, then turn the heat down slightly and let bubble to reduce by about a quarter. Season the reduced mixture with salt and pepper to taste.

Meanwhile, put the breadcrumbs in a bowl, add the Parmesan, parsley and some pepper, and toss with your fingers to combine.

Pour the mustardy crème fraîche over the asparagus, then scatter the crumb mixture on top, distributing it evenly. Drizzle over the rest of the melted butter. Bake the gratin on the middle shelf of the oven for 20 minutes. The top should be crisp and golden and the cream should be bubbling up around the sides of the dish. Sprinkle with the remaining thyme leaves and serve.

It is important not to overcook this dish – the asparagus should retain a bite and nuttiness. Overcooking could make the spears seem as though they have come out of a tin.

Grilled rump of lamb with asparagus and a salsa verde of lovage

The vast and wild lovage plant that looms over one corner of our vegetable garden seems to grow taller every day, no matter how much we cut it down to use in the kitchen. To me, lovage has a strong and very English taste – like peppery celery. It is good used sparingly in soups and salads, or as here, coarsely chopped in a green sauce to be spooned over grilled lamb. Be aware though that its flavour can easily be overpowering. This is a nice dish to eat outdoors on a warm spring day.

Serves 4

4 rumps of lamb, each about 200g, trimmed of most fat

sea salt and freshly ground black pepper

olive oil, to oil

20 asparagus spears

1 tbsp extra virgin olive oil

Salsa verde

1 tbsp good-quality capers packed in salt, well rinsed

1 garlic clove, peeled and crushed

1 tbsp Dijon mustard

1½ tbsp red wine vinegar

12 lovage leaves

bunch of flat leaf parsley

handful of rocket leaves

200ml extra virgin olive oil

Lay the rumps of lamb on a board and season well all over with 1½ tbsp salt. It sounds like a lot of salt, but do use it all. Cover the lamb and leave to sit in the fridge for at least 24 hours, but up to 3 days is good. This will tenderise the meat and give it a wonderful seasoned flavour right to its very core.

Remove the meat from the fridge an hour before cooking, to allow it to return to room temperature. Brush off any excess salt.

Meanwhile, make the sauce, preferably by hand. Roughly chop the capers and place them in a bowl with the crushed garlic, mustard and wine vinegar. Wash the lovage, parsley and rocket, pat dry and chop fairly onely, ensuring that there is still plenty of texture. Add to the bowl with a pinch of salt and some pepper. Pour over the extra virgin olive oil and stir well to combine. Set aside.

When ready to cook, heat up your barbecue or grill. When it is really hot, rub the meat all over with olive oil. Grill or barbecue for just 4 minutes on one side without turning, then turn and cook for a further 4 minutes on the other side. The meat should have a lovely dark crust. Set aside to rest in a warm place for 10 minutes.

Meanwhile, cook the asparagus. Bring a large pot of well-salted water to the boil. Snap the woody ends off the asparagus, and peel the lower part of the stalks. When the water is boiling vigorously, drop in the asparagus and cook for 1½ minutes or until it is just tender to the bite. Drain and dress with the extra virgin olive oil and season with salt and pepper.

Slice each lamb rump into 3 slices on the diagonal. Divide the asparagus among warm serving plates, lay the lamb on top and spoon over the salsa verde. Serve while still warm.

Cherries

The arrival of the first cherries marks the beginning of summer for me. In season from around June, cherries – along with apricots – are the first of the year's stone fruits to ripen. Yet strangely enough, cherries always remind me of Christmas, salt water and mangoes. As a child growing up in Australia, my memories of Christmas are of heat, long summer holidays by the sea, and boxes brimming with cherries and mangoes that my mother would bring home from the local greengrocers. My sister, brother and I would work through the first box of cherries in one sitting, our mother having shooed us outside so as not to make a mess. We'd gorge on handfuls of fruit, spitting the stones as far as we possibly could. I always hoped that one of those far-flung stones would miraculously grow into a tree that would produce endless fruit just for us ... but of course that never happened. I loved the taste of the sweet fragrant fruit, and my first ever pair of earrings was a pair of cherries hooked over the top of my ears!

There are more than 500 varieties of cherries in cultivation – their colours ranging from deep, dark red through pale yellow hues tinged with orange, to almost white. They can be broadly classified into sweet and sour cherries. My favourites lie among the paler varieties, whose flavour – even when perfectly ripe – has a gentle tartness. The darker varieties are juicy and wonderfully fragrant at their peak, but they seem to pass this point quickly and their flavour is soon overblown.

◊

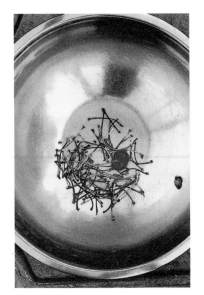

When you are buying cherries, look for fruit that is bright, plump and glossy, with flesh that is tight and plump. At farmers' markets and greengrocers they are often sold loose, so take time to pick through and take only the perfect ones. Check the stems, too – these should be green and crisp, not brown and woody. That said, the best way of finding out whether you've come across a good crop is to taste one.

◊

At the restaurant we use both sweet and sour cherries. Of the sour varieties, morello is a particular favourite. We pickle these small, tart, deep red cherries in a solution of sherry or wine vinegar, sugar and cloves, and keep them tightly sealed in a dark corner. In the early autumn, we serve them alongside cured meats or tossed through warm salads. Game, such as grouse or pheasant, and the early bitter winter leaves pair well with pickled cherries, as do the first of the autumn nuts – young soft walnuts and hazelnuts.

◊

When perfectly ripe and deliciously juicy, sweet cherries need no embellishment. If you can resist eating them straight from the bag, give them a quick rinse and savour them just as they are. Their season is brief – perhaps the briefest of all the summer fruits – lasting not much longer than a month, so make the most of them. Beyond enjoying them in their natural state, we also make sweet cherries into sorbets and ice creams, simple cordials and tarts. To round off a simple, satisfying meal, I really can't think of anything better than a plate of fresh ripe cherries and juicy apricots with soft, lemony goat's cheeses, drizzled lightly with fragrant honey.

Pickled cherries

We tend to make these with sour morello cherries, which we grow against the south-facing wall of our vegetable garden. Inedible raw, they are perfect for preserving. Over time, they become quite wrinkly in the pickling liquor, which I rather like. If you cannot get hold of these little sour cherries, pickle one of the sweet varieties instead.

Makes 2–3 x 500ml jars

1kg ripe cherries, preferably the sour morello variety

700g caster sugar

800ml red wine vinegar

6 bay leaves

12 cloves

15 black peppercorns

Discard any blemished or bruised fruit, but leave the stems on as they look really pretty. Rinse the cherries and pat dry.

Dissolve the sugar in the wine vinegar in a large saucepan over a low heat, then add the bay leaves, cloves and peppercorns. Bring to the boil, lower the heat and simmer for 10 minutes. Remove from the heat and allow the syrup to cool completely.

Pack the cherries loosely into warm sterilised jars and pour over the cooled syrup. Leave in a cool, dark cupboard for a couple of weeks before eating to allow the flavours to mellow, then refrigerate. They will keep in the fridge for up to a year.

Little clusters of grapes can be pickled in the same way. Proceed as above, adding 4 or 5 juniper berries to the pickling liquor. These grapes are lovely served with soft cheeses (see page 220).

Warm pheasant salad with tardivo, pickled cherries and toasted hazelnuts

This is a lovely autumn salad. Warm, torn pheasant is delicious served with the first bittersweet leaves of the year, new season's nut oil, pickled cherries and finely sliced fennel or celery to give a clean, watery crunch.

Serves 4

1 pheasant, about 1.2kg

sea salt and freshly ground black pepper

25ml olive oil

1 tardivo or radicchio, or a small bunch each of rocket and pissenlit (dandelion)

1 fennel bulb

1 pomegranate

1¹/2 tbsp aged balsamic vinegar

1¹/2 tbsp extra virgin olive oil

few drops of lemon juice

small handful of chervil leaves, finely chopped

Dressing

1 tbsp pickling liquor (from the cherries)

1 tbsp Dijon mustard

2 tsp sherry vinegar

60ml hazelnut oil

30ml mild-tasting extra virgin olive oil

To serve

about 12 pickled cherries (see page 29)

20 hazelnuts, lightly toasted and roughly chopped (optional)

Preheat the oven to 180°C/Gas 4. Cut off the tips of the pheasant wings, using a sharp knife. Season the bird generously all over. Heat the olive oil in a large non-stick pan over a low heat and pan-fry the pheasant, turning until golden brown all over.

Lay the bird on one side in a shallow roasting pan and roast in the oven for 10 minutes, then turn onto the other side and roast for a further 10 minutes. Now turn the bird breast side down and roast for a final 10 minutes or until cooked. To check, pull a leg away from the breast and look for any sign of rawness; also make sure that the juices run clear. Set aside to rest, breast side down, for 15 minutes.

Meanwhile, for the salad, separate the tardivo leaves, wash and gently pat dry, then place in a bowl. Remove the outer fibrous layer from the fennel, halve the bulb lengthways, then slice into very fine shards. Add to the leaves. Cut the pomegranate in half, then hold, cut side down, over a bowl and tap to release the seeds, picking out any bits of membrane that fall into the bowl. Scatter over the leaves.

For the dressing, whisk the pickling liquor, mustard, sherry vinegar and a pinch each of salt and pepper together in a bowl. Gradually whisk in the oils, then taste and adjust the seasoning if necessary. You should have a slightly sweet, nutty, earthy vinaigrette.

While still warm, tear the pheasant flesh from the bones and place in a bowl. Toss with the balsamic vinegar, olive oil, lemon juice, a little salt and pepper, and the chervil.

Now add the warm pheasant to the salad leaves and drizzle over a little of the dressing. Toss together lightly, using your fingertips, and arrange on serving plates. Scatter over the pickled cherries and toasted hazelnuts if using, drizzle with a little more vinaigrette and serve at once.

Clafoutis

When cherries are in season and really ripe, make this lovely light, comforting pudding. Don't bother to remove the stones – they make for a better flavour and are easily removed on eating.

Serves 6

40g unsalted butter

600g sweet cherries, washed and stems removed

100g caster sugar, plus 3 tbsp

1/2 tsp ground cinnamon

grated zest of 1 unwaxed lemon

2 organic free-range eggs, separated

75g plain flour

75g ground almonds

1 tsp vanilla extract

100ml double cream

pinch of sea salt

Melt the butter in a small saucepan over a medium heat. When it is foaming (but not browned), add the cherries, 100g sugar, the cinnamon and lemon zest. Cook gently for 10 minutes or until the cherries are soft, stirring gently from time to time. The juices should have reduced and thickened slightly. Remove from the heat.

Using a slotted spoon, spoon two-thirds of the fruit over the bottom of a shallow 23cm round baking tin; reserve the rest of the cherries in the juice for serving.

Preheat the oven to 200°C/Gas 6. Beat the egg yolks and remaining 3 tbsp sugar together in a large bowl until light and fluffy. Beat in the flour, ground almonds, vanilla extract and cream. In a separate clean bowl, whisk the egg whites with a pinch of salt until they form soft peaks.

Carefully fold the whisked egg whites into the batter until they are just evenly incorporated, then pour the mixture over the cherries. Bake on the top shelf of the oven for about 20 minutes until the batter is puffed and golden brown.

Let the clafoutis cool slightly for 5 minutes or so before serving, topped with the reserved cherries and juice.

I add a little salt to many of the desserts that I make, because I find it keeps the sweetness in check and pulls back fruits to their real flavour, which sugar has a tendency to mask.

Vanilla ice cream with poached cherries and chocolate sauce

Cherries, chocolate and vanilla ice cream seem to me to belong together, so I've combined them here to make a simple, light-hearted dessert. You could add some sliced banana and toasted chopped nuts for a sundae if you like. The ice cream can be made a day or two ahead, but preferably no longer.

Serves 6

Vanilla ice cream
450ml double cream
150ml whole milk
1 vanilla pod, split lengthways
6 organic free-range egg yolks
120g caster sugar

Poached cherries
500g cherries
200g caster sugar
juice of 1 lemon
1 tbsp Pedro Ximenez sherry

Chocolate sauce
125g good-quality dark, bitter chocolate (minimum 68% cocoa solids), grated
125ml double cream
125ml whole milk
1 tsp honey

To finish
handful of cherries with stalks, washed

To make the ice cream, pour the cream and milk into a heavy-based pan and place over a low heat. Scrape the vanilla seeds from the pod and add them to the creamy milk with the empty pod. Slowly bring to just below the boil, remove from the heat and set aside to infuse for 15 minutes.

In the meantime, beat the egg yolks and sugar together in a large bowl with a whisk until pale. Gently reheat the creamy milk and pour on to the egg yolk mixture, stirring with the whisk as you do so. Return to the pan.

Stir the custard over the lowest possible heat until it thickens. This will take 8–10 minutes (don't be tempted to increase the heat, or the custard will curdle). As soon as it is thick enough to lightly coat the back of a wooden spoon, remove from the heat and pour into a bowl. Allow to cool, then churn in an ice-cream maker until thick. Unless using straight away, transfer to a plastic container and store in the freezer.

For the poached cherries, rinse the fruit, remove the stems and place in a saucepan with the sugar and lemon juice. Bring to a simmer, then cover and poach gently for 10 minutes until the cherries are very tender and have released a lot of liquid. Using a slotted spoon, transfer the cherries to a bowl. Add the sherry to the pan, turn up the heat and boil vigorously for 2 minutes. Pour over the fruit and let cool slightly (while you make the sauce) or leave until cold.

For the chocolate sauce, combine all the ingredients in a saucepan and heat gently, stirring until smooth. Remove from the heat and cool slightly.

To serve, layer the vanilla ice cream, poached cherries and warm chocolate sauce alternately in pretty glasses. Top with a few fresh cherries and serve at once.

Cherry granita

This lovely, vibrant, fairy floss pink granita is the perfect end to a simple lunch on a warm day in June. The sweet icy granules tingle on your tongue, releasing a taste that is pure cherry. The fruit is uncooked in this recipe, allowing the cleanest possible flavour of cherry to shine through.

Serves 6–8

1.5kg ripe, sweet cherries
400g caster sugar
250ml water
small pinch of sea salt
squeeze of lemon juice

Wash the cherries and pat dry, then remove the stems and stones. Tip the fruit into a food processor and purée until smooth. Pass through a sieve into a bowl and set aside.

Place the sugar and water in a heavy-based pan over a medium heat. Once the sugar has dissolved, turn up the heat slightly and simmer for 3–4 minutes or until the syrup is slightly viscous. Remove from the heat and allow to cool completely.

When cold, pour the syrup over the puréed cherries. Add the salt, squeeze in a few drops of lemon juice and stir well to combine. Pour into a shallow freezerproof tray – the purée should be no more than 3cm thick. Cover and place in the freezer for an hour or so.

When the granita begins to set and has firmed up around the edges, remove from the freezer and use a fork to drag the frozen crystals from the edges in towards the centre. Don't beat the mixture – a granita is meant to be icy and crunchy, not smooth like a sorbet.

Return to the freezer for a further 30 minutes or so, then repeat the procedure. Now freeze until set. Store in a covered plastic container in the freezer until ready to use. To serve, scrape shavings from the granita and pile into chilled glasses.

Perfectly ripe fruit is generally better showcased in a granita rather than a sorbet, because the latter requires more sugar to set smoothly and the more sugar that is added, the more the true flavour of the fruit is masked.

Brandied cherries

These little translucent ruby jewels shine from their glass jars, giving a sense of comfort and warmth to everyone who sets eyes on them. Every year we lay a few fruits in brandy – usually cherries, damsons and raspberries – primarily so that we can enjoy their taste and beauty a little longer than their natural season allows. The brandy will eventually overwhelm the delicate flavour of the fruit, but if kept in the fridge they will last for a year. Choose fruit in really good condition, without bruises, soft spots or blemishes.

Makes 1kg

1kg ripe, sweet cherries

400ml good-quality brandy, such as an aged apple brandy

125g caster sugar

120ml water

Wash the cherries, leaving on their stems and lay them out to dry on a clean cloth.

Pour the brandy into a small saucepan and add the sugar and water. Heat gently to dissolve the sugar and warm the liquor.

Pack the cherries loosely into one large sterilised jar or a couple of smaller ones. Pour the warmed brandy over the cherries, making sure that the fruit is totally submerged in the alcohol. Seal and store in a cool dark place for a week or so to allow the flavours to develop, then store in the fridge.

We use brandied cherries in a variety of sweet and savoury dishes: with quail, pigeon or pâté, bitter leaves and autumn nuts; warmed through and served with duck breast; with thinly sliced raw fennel, toasted hazelnuts and a rich, creamy cheese, such as robiola; sautéed quickly in a pan with a little butter, a touch of sugar and some syrup from the jar to tumble warm over vanilla ice cream; with grilled fresh apricots and a dollop of sweetened mascarpone; paired with chunks of dark chocolate and a biscotti or two, for an elegant, lazy dessert.

Cherry cordial

I love making cordials, as they are celebratory in feel and look beautiful served in jugs on the table for everyone to share. You can adapt this simple recipe to almost any seasonal fruit, including quince, gooseberries, blackcurrants, raspberries and blackberries.

Makes about 1 litre

1kg ripe, sweet cherries
320g caster sugar
pared zest of 1 unwaxed lemon
1 litre water
1 tbsp rose syrup

To serve
still or sparkling water
crushed ice

Wash the cherries and pat dry, then remove the stems. Tip the fruit into a medium heavy-based pan and add the sugar, lemon zest and water. Bring to the boil over a medium heat, then turn the heat down and simmer gently for 15 minutes or until the cherries are tender and have bled their colour into the water. Remove from the heat and allow to cool slightly.

Strain through a fine chinois into a bowl, pressing down on the fruit with the back of a ladle to extract as much juice as possible. Let the strained syrup cool completely, then add the rose syrup and stir well to combine. Pour into a sterilised bottle or jar and store in the fridge for up to a week.

To serve, dilute the cordial with still or fizzy water, as you prefer, and serve with lots of crushed ice on a hot day.

Fish & shellfish

I love fish of all description. Their clean, clear flavours appeal to me and I've become increasingly confident in cooking them. The variety is endless, from spanking fresh oily fish – like sardines, mackerel and anchovies – to the more subtle white-fleshed species – such as halibut, bass, bream and sole. The largest of the white flatfish, turbot – affectionately known as the king of the sea – can be considered somewhat in between in the kitchen. It has rich, succulent white flesh that can take the intense flavours of porcini, girolles, or even bone marrow.

I am particularly fond of shellfish, especially juicy king scallops, sweet crab from the Dorset coast and our luscious native lobsters. And I love the way mussels and clams add their distinctive flavour to everything they come into contact with. Bread is an essential partner to these bivalves – to mop up every trace of their delicious briny juices.

Just as all things worth eating have a time and place in which they are at their very best, so does fish. Lobster, for example, is beautiful in the spring and autumn when its flesh is firm and sweet. Mussels are at their prime in the autumn. Their beautiful appearance and plump, orange flesh – tasting of the sea – makes me eager to devour them. They work well with strong, clear flavours, such as ripe tomatoes, chilli, garlic, rosemary and wine vinegar. Surprisingly though, mussels are equally good with the delicate flavours of saffron, white wine and crème fraîche. Clams too, though they can seem fiddly to eat, lend a superb flavour to the most basic of dishes. Linguine with vongole (clams), for example, is merely pasta tossed with clams, garlic, a little dried chilli, a splash of white wine and lashings of good grassy olive oil... yet it is a dish fit for a king.

There is much to say on the virtues of our other shellfish – noble lobster and delicate crab, of course, but also beautiful scallops, with their plump sweet flesh. I love to eat them griddled with garlicky butter or tossed with an array of winter leaves. Poole prawns that arrive in September are another favourite. These are so tiny and full of flavour, they need nothing more than a squeeze of lemon juice, a sprinkling of salt and perhaps a few slivers of fresh red chilli.

◊

As for oily fish – anchovies, sardines, mackerel and herring – these are delicious without question, as long as they are very fresh. Their lovely, oily flesh spoils quickly, so they need to be eaten soon after you buy them – preferably the same day, or at least within 24 hours. They also need to be served piping hot. Vinegar cuts through their strong flavours successfully, as does horseradish, and a sweet foil of tomatoes or beetroot and a sprinkling of salt is vital for these fish.

◊

Wild halibut, caught off the coast of Scotland, is quite simply the cleanest and whitest of all fish, with a beautiful texture. It marries well with just about anything – from tandoor spices to a simple accompaniment of spinach dressed with olive oil and a good squeeze of lemon. Wild salmon, in season from mid-spring through early summer, is only ever a rare treat. Its deep orangey pink flesh has a delicate richness, which I adore. Baked whole in salt, it is a delight served with freshly made mayonnaise and young peppery rocket, or the first new potatoes of the year pulled straight from the ground – and perhaps a plate of sliced ripe tomatoes.

Turbot – rich and gelatinous – is a different beast altogether. It benefits from being cooked on the bone and can carry stronger flavours. One way to cook it is with porcini mushrooms, sourdough

breadcrumbs and bone marrow – a lovely elegant dish to serve in the colder months. And then there is wild bass and bream, and beautiful red mullet with its distinctive flavour of the sea… so many tempting options.

Lastly I must not forget monkfish, the great pretender, known as poor man's lobster in France because its flesh is more reminiscent of a crustacean than a white fish. Firm, meaty and bouncy, with only one central bone to remove, it is delicious served with white beans laced with tomatoes and tarragon, or in a rustic fish stew.

◊

The wealth of the sea is truly breathtaking and seemingly endless, which brings me to one final, very important consideration. Of this rich bounty we must take care, for its ecosystem has become so very fragile. The waters of the world have been ruthlessly overfished and supplies are dwindling on a frightening scale. We must take from them wisely and carefully – sustainably. I urge you to seek out fish that have been line caught, close to our shores. Ask your fishmonger where his fish has come from – has it been caught by local day boats rather than deep-sea trawlers? Steer clear of species during their spawning season, and at other times avoid taking too much of any one of them. Be aware of endangered species – wild salmon, halibut, monkfish etc. – and eat them rarely. It is vital, so that we – and those who come after us – may be able to continue to enjoy them…

We use hand-dived scallops at the restaurant, each one individually picked by someone, as opposed to trawled in nets that are dragged along the bottom of the sea, damaging just about everything they come into contact with.

Poole prawns with chilli, salt and lemon

Available for just one month of the year – September – and named after Poole in Dorset where they come from, these are possibly the most delicious little prawns in the world. We deep-fry them in the hottest oil until crunchy and eat them whole – piping hot and sprinkled generously with salt. I encourage you to do the same – please don't bother to peel them as the flavour is all in the shell.

20–30 prawns per person (sounds a lot, but they are tiny)

corn oil, for deep-frying

sea salt

1 red chilli, deseeded and finely sliced (optional)

generous squeeze of lemon juice

Rinse the prawns and pat thoroughly dry with kitchen paper. Heat the corn oil in a deep-fat fryer or other suitable heavy-based pan to 170°C; check the temperature with a cook's thermometer.

Cook the prawns in several batches: add to the hot oil and cook for 1–2 minutes until bright red in colour and crunchy in texture. Remove with a slotted spoon and drain on kitchen paper while you deep-fry the rest. Season generously with sea salt and scatter over the sliced chilli if using. Finish with a good squeeze of lemon juice.

These crunchy prawns are delicious as a pre-dinner nibble with a glass of Prosecco or Champagne.

My choice of oil for deep-frying is corn oil, because it cooks evenly and has a neutral taste that doesn't interfere with the taste of the food I am cooking.

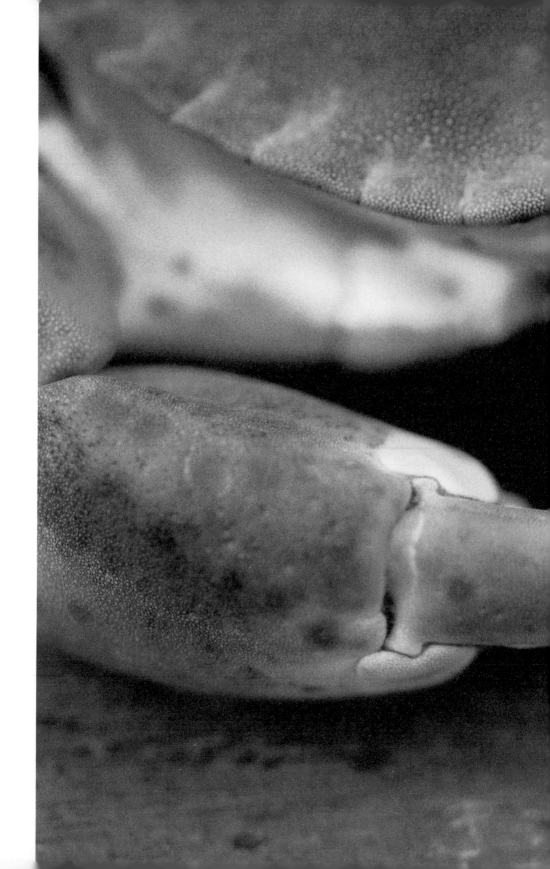

Crab cakes with corn purée and chilli oil

These little, light crab cakes are unusual in that they are simply white crab meat flavoured with a few aromatics and bound with rich, unctuous homemade mayonnaise. They sing of summer, especially when served with a purée of sweet, fresh corn – the perfect foil for richly flavoured crab. Add a squeeze of lime and a drizzle of chilli oil to make this dish just about perfect!

Makes 8 little cakes

250g fresh picked white crab meat

1 red chilli, deseeded and finely diced

1 tbsp finely chopped coriander leaves

100ml homemade mayonnaise (see page 182; use the juice of 1 lemon and omit the vinegar)

squeeze of lime or lemon juice

sea salt

50g fresh white breadcrumbs

150g unsalted butter

Chilli oil

1 red chilli, deseeded and finely diced

80ml extra virgin olive oil

Corn purée

3 fresh corn cobs, outer husks removed

120ml water

40g unsalted butter

2 tsp sugar

sea salt and freshly ground black pepper

50ml crème fraîche

1 tsp Tabasco, or to taste

To serve

lime wedges

Put the crab meat into a bowl, add the chilli and coriander and fork through to distribute evenly. Add the mayonnaise and stir well to combine – it not only enriches the flavour of the crab, but also binds it together. Add a squeeze of lime or lemon juice and enough salt to bring out all the flavours. Form the mixture into 8 little cakes and place on a tray. Chill for 30 minutes to firm up slightly.

Spread the breadcrumbs evenly on a board and roll the crab cakes in them to coat generously. Cover and refrigerate until needed.

For the chilli oil, put the diced chilli into a bowl, add a good pinch of salt and pour on the olive oil. Stir to combine and leave to infuse.

For the corn purée, cut the kernels from the cobs. The easiest way to do this is to stand the cob upright on a board and run a sharp knife down in sections. Discard any stringy bits. Tip the corn kernels into a saucepan, add the water, butter and sugar, and season generously with salt and pepper. Cover and cook gently over a medium heat until the corn is tender, about 20–25 minutes, then drain, reserving the liquor.

Transfer half of the corn to a bowl, using a slotted spoon. Tip the rest into a blender or food processor and blend until smooth. Pass through a chinois into a bowl to ensure a really smooth purée; if it is too thick, stir in a little of the reserved liquor. Add to the rest of the corn and stir well. Add the crème fraîche and Tabasco and stir again. Check the seasoning and keep warm.

To cook the crab cakes, heat the butter in a wide non-stick pan over a medium-low heat. When it is warm, gently lay the crab cakes in the pan and cook for about 2 minutes on each side until golden and crispy. Remove with a slotted spoon and drain on kitchen paper.

Serve the crab cakes piping hot, with the corn purée. Pass around the chilli oil and lime wedges for squeezing.

Lobster salad with fennel and blood oranges

The clean crunch of fennel and winter leaves, such as Castelfranco or frisée, complement the sweet, rich flesh of lobster in this winter salad, and the sweet, citric taste of blood oranges rounds off the dish perfectly. Crab also works well here, so you could substitute it for the lobster. These quantities are sufficient for a starter; to serve as a lunch or main course, allow one lobster each.

Serves 4

2 very fresh, live lobsters, each about 500g

sea salt and freshly ground black pepper

1/2 lemon

50ml mild-tasting extra virgin olive oil (such as Sicilian or Ligurian)

3 blood oranges

1/2 Castelfranco lettuce or frisée

1 fennel bulb

bunch of young, tender agretti or rocket

small bunch of chervil, stems removed

aged balsamic vinegar, to drizzle

Keep the lobsters covered with a damp cloth in the fridge and cook soon after buying. An hour or so before cooking, place them in the freezer – the intense cold will send them into a deep sleep.

When ready to cook the lobsters, put a large pot of well-salted water on to boil – it should be almost as salty as the sea. When it comes to a rolling boil, drop in the lobsters and cook for 8 minutes exactly. The timing is important, as lobster meat is not at all good if it is overcooked. Remove the lobsters from the pan with a pair of tongs and set aside until they are cool enough to handle.

To remove the meat from the shell, first twist off the claws and tap the thickest part of these with a rolling pin to crack them open. Gently remove the claw shell, leaving the flesh intact if possible and reserve for serving. Now lay the body on its back on a board and, using a very sharp, large knife, cut through the middle of the soft underbelly to slice the tail meat in half lengthways. You should then be able to remove the outer shell (rather like removing a coat). Season the flesh with a squeeze of lemon juice, a drizzle of olive oil and a little salt and pepper.

Using a paring knife, cut away the skin and white pith from the blood oranges, then slice crossways into 3mm thick pinwheels. Separate the Castelfranco or frisée leaves, leaving small ones whole and roughly tearing larger ones, then wash and gently pat dry. Remove the tough outer layer of the fennel bulb, then halve lengthways. Now slice each half lengthways into fine slices and squeeze over a few drops of lemon juice to stop them discolouring.

To assemble the salad, place the fennel, Castelfranco or frisée, agretti or rocket, and chervil leaves in a bowl with the lobster meat and toss lightly. Dress with the remaining lemon juice and olive oil. Taste and season with salt and pepper if needed.

Divide the salad among serving plates and arrange the blood orange slices on top. Finish with the reserved lobster claw flesh and drizzle with a little aged balsamic to serve.

Carpaccio of smoked haddock with chilli and winter purslane

Finely sliced, very fresh fish served raw with a few carefully chosen flavourings makes a beautifully simple, elegant first course. The tastes here are clean and as light as air – so subtle that they linger for barely a moment before they evaporate. The seasoning needs to be quite generous – it is delicious to come across a crystally crunch of salt.

Serves 4

400g very fresh (undyed) smoked haddock fillet

juice of 1 lemon

4 tbsp very good-quality olive oil

1 red chilli, finely sliced

coarse sea salt

handful of purslane (or pea shoots or cress)

Lay the smoked haddock skin side down on a board. Now, using a very sharp knife, slice downwards at an angle through to the skin to cut into wafer-thin slices. As you cut, lay the haddock slices on a plate – overlapping them as you do so.

Sprinkle with the lemon juice, drizzle with the olive oil and scatter over the chilli. Season with salt to taste.

Finish with the purslane – not too much, as it should be little more than a palate-cleansing crunch. Serve immediately, before the lemon juice has a chance to 'cook' the fish...

The gentle flavour of sweet smoky haddock is better experienced in its raw state in my view. I find the delicate texture of the raw flesh matches the ethereal flavour of the fish more appropriately.

Roasted halibut with preserved lemon and crème fraîche sauce

This combination of simply roasted firm-fleshed, white fish and preserved lemon is unfussy – both in its execution and taste, but it is very, very good! In late summer I love to eat it with sliced perfectly ripe tomatoes, drizzled with very good olive oil. In the cooler months, I like it with spinach – just wilted and flavoured with a little finely sliced chilli and a drizzle of olive oil.

Serves 4

4 halibut fillets, about 180g each, with skin

1 tbsp olive oil

sea salt and freshly ground black pepper

Sauce

2 preserved lemons

small bunch of mint, leaves only

small bunch of basil, leaves only

3 tbsp water

squeeze of lemon juice (if needed)

200ml crème fraîche

To serve

lemon wedges

First make the sauce. Cut the preserved lemons into quarters and rinse under cold running water, removing and discarding the flesh, which can taste bitter. You will be left with just the peel. Place this in a blender along with the herbs and water, and purée to a smooth paste. Transfer to a bowl and try a little – it should taste fragrant and distinctive, a little salty but not excessively so. If it seems a bit too salty, add a squeeze or two of lemon juice, otherwise don't bother. Stir in the crème fraîche and set aside in the fridge while you cook the fish.

Preheat the oven to 180°C/Gas 4. Place a large non-stick ovenproof pan over a medium heat and add the olive oil. Season the fish generously with salt and pepper, seasoning the skin more than the flesh side. Once the pan is hot, lay the fish in it, skin side down. Cook, without touching or turning, for about 2 minutes until the skin is golden and has popped itself up from the base of the pan. Now place the pan in the oven (still without turning the fish) and cook for 4 minutes.

Remove from the oven (remembering to protect your hand with an oven glove as the pan handle will be very hot). Lift the fish onto serving plates, placing the fillets skin side up. Spoon the cool lemony sauce on top and serve straight away, with lemon wedges and whatever else you choose!

Never overcrowd a pan, especially when cooking fish. Food needs space and air around it to cook properly. If you think your pan might not be big enough, then use two pans or cook in batches. An overcrowded pan will only lead to food that is stewed … and its final taste will reflect that.

Salt-baked wild salmon with roasted tomato aïoli, potatoes and purslane

This is a really good way to cook fish that is to be served whole for a large gathering. It allows a rich gelatinous, slightly oily fish to benefit from all the wonderful flavours that come from the bones. The salt coating sets firm, like clay, when it is mixed with water and exposed to high heat, so the fish steams beautifully inside its protective cask. Ask your fishmonger to gut the fish but leave the scales on – they will prevent the salt from penetrating the fish as it cooks.

Serves 8–12

1 wild salmon, about 4kg, gutted but not scaled

2 unwaxed lemons, thinly sliced

1 branch of wild fennel

5kg coarse rock salt

Tomato aïoli

3 organic free-range egg yolks

2 garlic cloves, peeled and crushed

juice of 1/2 lemon

sea salt and freshly ground black pepper

6–8 slow-roasted tomatoes (see page 123), cooled

80ml extra virgin olive oil

Potatoes

1kg young English new potatoes, such as Red Duke, washed

juice of 1/2 lemon

60ml extra virgin olive oil

handful of purslane or pea shoots

Start by making the aïoli. Place the egg yolks in a blender or food processor, add the garlic, lemon juice, a little salt and pepper and the tomatoes, then whiz briefly to combine. With the motor running, pour in the olive oil in a slow, steady stream through the feeder tube. Taste and adjust the seasoning if necessary. (This can be made up to a day in advance.)

When you are ready to cook the salmon, preheat the oven to its highest setting, at least 250°C/Gas 9. Rinse the fish inside and out under cold running water, then pat it dry. Place the lemon slices inside the cavity, along with the wild fennel, but don't bother to season the fish.

Put the rock salt in a mixing bowl and add enough cold water to give the consistency of wet sand (around as much as a litre, depending on the type of salt). Mix together with your hands.

Spread half of the salt mix on a large baking tray or in a shallow roasting pan to create a flat, even surface. Lay the fish on top and cover with the rest of the salt, packing it firmly around the fish (as if you were burying someone at the beach!).

Place on the middle shelf of the hot oven and bake for 20 minutes or until the fish is barely cooked. To test, pierce the thickest part of the fish through to the bone with a sharp knife. If the knife tip feels warm to the touch as you withdraw it, the fish is ready; if not, cook it for a little longer. Set aside to rest and cool to room temperature; the fish will continue to cook in the residual heat as it cools within its salt crust.

Meanwhile, cook the potatoes in well-salted boiling water until very tender (almost falling apart), about 20–25 minutes. Drain and while still warm, sprinkle with the lemon juice, season with lots of pepper and a little more salt if necessary, and add the olive oil. Toss well to combine, then add the purslane or pea shoots and toss again.

To serve, crack the salt crust open with the handle of a knife or a rolling pin. Carefully remove the salt and peel off the skin from the fish. Serve the beautiful, succulent flesh warm or at room temperature, with the warm potatoes and tomato aïoli.

Use a coarse, crystally rock or sea salt but not Maldon as it is too fine and expensive. You can buy 25kg sacks of rock salt from good fishmongers, or the cash and carry, which shouldn't cost you more than around £10 a bag.

Squid with peppers, red wine and wild marjoram

This beautifully coloured, richly flavoured stew calls for some good, open-textured peasant-style bread to mop up the juices. I also like to serve it with a generous dollop of aïoli (see page 168). I make this dish most often in early autumn when peppers are still good, but the chill that has crept into the air calls for a depth and warmth, which the red wine and wild marjoram provide.

Serves 4–6

1kg small squid, with tentacles

1 tsp fennel seeds

3 garlic cloves, peeled

1 dried red chilli

1 red pepper

1 yellow pepper

4 tbsp mild-tasting extra virgin olive oil

2 red onions, peeled and finely sliced

few strips of orange zest

small bunch of marjoram

10 (or so) little ripe tomatoes, such as small San Marzano or datterini

250ml good-quality red wine

sea salt and freshly ground black pepper

Start by cleaning the squid. Hold the body with one hand and pull out the head with the tentacles attached, using the other hand; most of the innards will come too. Cut the tentacles from the head, discarding the head. Remove the transparent quill from the body and the soft gooey matter. Rinse the body pouch and tentacles gently under cold running water, drain and set aside in a cool place.

Toast the fennel seeds in a dry non-stick frying pan over a medium heat until they begin to pop and release their aroma. Meanwhile, pound the garlic using a pestle and mortar. Add the warm fennel seeds and dried chilli and pound to crush and combine with the garlic. Cut the peppers in half lengthways, remove the pith, then slice into 2.5cm strips; set aside.

Warm 2 tbsp of the olive oil in a heavy-based wide pan over a low heat and cook the onion gently for 10 minutes until it is soft and sweet. Add the pounded mixture, stir to combine and cook for a couple of minutes. Now add the orange zest, sliced peppers, marjoram and small whole ripe tomatoes.

Pour in the wine and turn up the heat slightly, so that it sizzles. Add a good pinch of salt and a grinding or two of pepper. Turn down the heat, place a lid on the pan and cook gently for 30 minutes or so or until the peppers are soft. You should by now have a beautifully coloured stew with a deep, warm satisfying rich smell!

Heat the remaining 2 tbsp olive oil in a frying pan. Season the squid generously. In batches if necessary, cook the squid in the hot pan over a high heat without turning for a minute or so, then turn and cook briefly on the other side. Throw the tentacles in last of all as they take very little time to cook.

Tip the cooked squid into the hot stew and stir over the heat for a minute or so to combine the flavours. Ladle into shallow soup bowls and serve piping hot with bread.

Monkfish curry with coconut, lime and curry leaves

I like making curries. I find it interesting and fun to build and balance the flavours – sweet, sour, salty, pungent, hot and, above all, clean and pure. Fresh curry leaves lend the most wonderful taste – just the smell of them transports me somewhere hot and exciting. Monkfish is a good choice of fish for curries and wet dishes – its firm, white, meaty flesh is a clean foil for more complex flavours.

Serves 4–6

1 tbsp unsalted butter or ghee

2 red onions, peeled and finely sliced

2 tsp mustard seeds

2 tsp fennel seeds

1 tsp coriander seeds

bunch of coriander, roots and stems finely chopped, leaves reserved

2 garlic cloves, peeled and crushed

2 red chillies, chopped (seeds left in)

6 fresh curry leaves

2 kaffir lime leaves

juice of 2 limes

2 tbsp fish sauce

1 tbsp palm sugar or caster sugar

2 x 340g jars (or tinned) good-quality peeled plum tomatoes

800g monkfish fillet

400ml tin coconut milk

lime wedges, to serve

Place a large heavy-based saucepan over a medium-low heat. Add the butter and, once it begins to melt, add the sliced onions. Cook over a low heat for 10 minutes, stirring from time to time.

Meanwhile, toast the mustard, fennel and coriander seeds in a dry non-stick frying pan over a medium heat until the spices begin to pop and release their aroma. Be careful not to burn them or they will make the curry taste bitter. Remove from the heat and, while still warm, pound to a rough powder using a pestle and mortar.

Add the ground spices to the cooked, sweet onions along with the chopped coriander root and stems, garlic, chillies and curry leaves. Crush the kaffir lime leaves between your fingers to help release their flavour and add to the pan. Cook for a further 5–6 minutes... your kitchen will smell deliciously fragrant.

Add the lime juice, fish sauce and sugar, stir once or twice and turn up the heat slightly. Add the tomatoes and cook for 15 minutes, stirring occasionally.

Now taste the curry base. The flavour should be warm, slightly sweet, but also sour – the spices should give a deep satisfying base note flavour, the coriander will give it a clean light finish. Pause and consider whether all those flavours are apparent. If not, add a little more lime juice perhaps, or a little more fish sauce to underpin the flavours with a saltiness if needed. This curry base will sit happily for a day or so in the fridge, if you would like to make it ahead.

To finish, warm the curry over a medium heat. Using a sharp knife, slice the monkfish into 2.5cm pieces (it will shrink slightly during cooking). When the curry is simmering, pour in the coconut milk, stir, then add the monkfish. Cook for 3–4 minutes until the fish is just cooked – it will feel firm to the touch.

Scatter over the reserved coriander leaves, ladle into bowls and serve with lime wedges and plain rice or, as I do, with grilled flat bread laced with toasted fennel seeds.

Olive oil

Probably the single most important ingredient I use in my kitchen is extra virgin olive oil. It enhances the flavours of nearly all our vegetable dishes and salads, as well as soups and simply grilled meat and fish.

Obtained from the first pressing of the olives, extra virgin olive oil can be robust – tasting peppery, nutty or grassy, sometimes even of hay! Other varieties can be light, fruity and elegant. The colour can range from deep murky olivey green to pale and golden, taking in all the shades in between. And the viscosity varies from light to medium; some oils are even dense and heavy. The price, too, can range from modest to wildly expensive.

You really need to try different olive oils, to find those you like the taste of and can comfortably afford. Look for labels indicating that the oil has been bottled on the estate on which the olives have been grown, hand-picked and pressed. This is usually a sign of superior quality.

Olives are picked in the autumn. It is only when they are properly ripe that harvesting can begin. The French claim that the 'oil is in the olive' only after St Catherine's day on 25th November, the Lebanese say that All Saints day on 1st November marks the date. Most farmers, however, will tell you that the best time to begin harvesting is after the first rain, when the olives become easier to pick. Olives harvested early produce oil that is stronger and greener in colour with the best health-giving properties, but the yield is generally lower, so many farmers prefer to wait a little longer. In my view, oils from olives picked early have the best flavour.

The finest olive oil is created when oil is extracted purely by cold pressing, with neither heat nor chemicals used in the extraction process. To be of fine quality, an oil must have less than one per cent oleic acidity. Any higher percentage could mean that the oil has been extracted from damaged or badly handled fruit.

◊

We use several olive oils in the restaurant, including a lovely, slightly grassy, green oil from a small estate in Friuli in Northern Italy, as well as oils from Provence and as far away as Lebanon. Occasionally we work with some punchy oils from Spain and the

Butter has its place in cooking – lending richness and a wonderful velvety smoothness. I do use it to cook with, but more often I will reach for a bottle of olive oil. It is, of course, much better for you than butter, but as always, taste to me is the most important thing – and the flavour of good olive oil is second to none.

very popular robust oils for which Tuscany is so famous. The one I love above all others though is the light, golden, delicate, very slightly fruity olive oil from Liguria. Made purely from a variety of olive known as *taggiasca*, it tastes wonderful and always gives me a feeling of utter contentment... making me smile.

Try different olive oils to discover your favourites. The best way to taste an olive oil is to pour a little into a glass and sip it (not directly out of your hand as is sometimes suggested). Let it roll around your tongue for a moment or two and take in the aroma from the glass. The overwhelming taste and smell, no matter how delicate, should be of the fruit from which it has been pressed.

◊

Controversially perhaps, I use good olive oil for all my cooking both at home and at the restaurant, with the exception of deep-frying, when I use corn oil. I feel that what you cook with should always taste good straight from the bottle – it is never merely a cooking medium to me. In cases where high temperature cooking is called for, I'll use a mild-tasting light olive oil rather than extra virgin. I tend to save the best extra virgin olive oils for dishes that I feel showcase the virtues of a full-flavoured oil. And, of course, an olive oil must sit happily alongside the flavours it is paired with.

◊

As for infused olive oils, I have yet to buy one that I think tastes good. Quick to oxidise and spoil, these oils do not taste vibrant and fresh to me. I prefer to infuse my own olive oil – in small quantities for immediate use. Delicate lemon-infused oil, known as *agrumato* in Italy, is my favourite...

◊

Lemon-infused olive oil Finely pare the zest from 3 lemons in wide strips using a swivel vegetable peeler, place in a small pan and pour on 250ml extra virgin olive oil (light in flavour, such as Ligurian). Warm gently to blood heat (around 37°C), for just 10 minutes, to release the lemon aroma. Remove from the heat and let stand for 30 minutes before using to enable the flavours to settle and become acquainted. Use on the day of making ideally, or within 24 hours.

◊

Like all beautiful things, extra virgin olive oil should be treated with respect and care. It does not respond well to heat, light or exposure to air, all of which cause it to oxidise. It really needs to be kept in a cool dark place – a cool larder is perfect – and used within 6 months. I occasionally keep a small bottle to hand by the stove but only because I know it will be used within a day or two...

Fragrant lemon-infused olive oil is lovely spooned over char-grilled chicken or fish, or drizzled over very fresh young sheep's or cow's milk curd.

Carpaccio of beef with red pepper relish

A well-executed carpaccio makes an elegant first course. It's also a lovely way to showcase the flavour of good-quality beef. Traditionally, carpaccio is simply finely sliced pounded beef, dressed with nothing more than salt, extra virgin olive oil and perhaps a few shavings of Parmesan. Here, I have paired it with a little more – summery red peppers and the lightest curd cheese. In winter we serve it with shavings of white truffle, deep-fried artichoke hearts, or slivers of white celery heart.

Serves 4 or 8

500g best-quality fillet of beef

extra virgin olive oil, to drizzle

sea salt

juice of 1/2 lemon, or to taste

Red pepper relish

1 large red pepper

40g currants

50g very fresh pine nuts

sea salt and freshly ground black pepper

1 small garlic clove, peeled and finely chopped

small bunch of basil, leaves only, finely chopped

small bunch of rocket, chopped

20ml sherry vinegar

1 tsp Pedro Ximénez sherry

50ml mild-tasting extra virgin olive oil

To serve

4 generous tbsp fromage blanc or other sweet young curd cheese

Trim the meat of any sinew or fat, then wrap and place in the freezer for about 20–30 minutes until thoroughly chilled but not frozen. (This will make it easier to slice.)

Cut 16 x 25cm squares of baking parchment. Using a very sharp knife, slice the meat with the grain into 8 slices. Brush one parchment square with a little olive oil and lay a slice of meat on top. Cover with a second oiled square of parchment. Working from the centre outwards, pound the meat evenly and gently using a wooden rolling pin. Keep pounding (but not too hard or you will tear the flesh) until the meat is no more than 3mm thick. When you have finished, the slice should be two or three times its original size. Continue until you have 8 slices of finished carpaccio. Refrigerate until ready to serve, but for no longer than 4 hours, or the meat will discolour and lose flavour.

To make the relish, roast the pepper under a hot grill, turning until the skin is charred all over. Transfer to a bowl, cover with cling film and let stand for 20 minutes. Preheat the oven to 180°C/Gas 4. Soak the currants in a little warm water for 15 minutes to soften. Warm the pine nuts in the oven for a few minutes to release their flavour.

Peel, halve and deseed the pepper, then cut into small dice and place in a bowl. Add the pine nuts. Squeeze out the excess water from the currants and add these too. Season and add the garlic, basil, rocket, sherry vinegar, sherry and finally the extra virgin olive oil. Stir well and let stand for a few minutes, then taste and adjust the seasoning. The relish should be slightly sweet, soft and fresh.

To assemble, carefully peel off one sheet of parchment paper from each parcel. Then lay a slice exposed side down on each chilled plate and peel off the top layer of paper. Add a second slice of beef to each plate if serving two each. Drizzle with the olive oil, season with salt and sprinkle with a few drops of lemon juice. Spoon over the relish, leaving most of the meat exposed. Finish with the fromage blanc and a final drizzle of relish. Serve immediately.

Ribollita

You will, no doubt, have seen this soup documented many times before. A much-loved dish from Tuscany, it consists of little more than reboiled beans, tomatoes, stale bread and cavolo nero – the beautiful black cabbage that hails from the region. My version replaces the bread with farro, but holds the tradition of finishing with lashings of beautiful peppery, grassy Tuscan oil. I often make this soup at home for my children – we let it sit on top of the stove and dip into it as we feel like it. To me this is ultimate comfort food ... good for you in the extreme.

Serves 6–8

400g dried cannellini beans, soaked in cold water overnight

about 3 litres water

3 tbsp olive oil

2 onions, peeled and chopped

1 dried red chilli, crumbled

sea salt and freshly ground black pepper

2 celery sticks, chopped

2 carrots, peeled and chopped

3 small garlic cloves, peeled and smashed

small bunch of sage

2 potatoes, peeled and chopped

150g farro, well rinsed under cold water

400g jar (or tin) good-quality peeled plum tomatoes

bunch of cavolo nero, thick stalks removed, roughly chopped

extra virgin olive oil, preferably Tuscan, to serve

Drain the beans and place them in a heavy-based saucepan. Pour on about 2 litres water to cover generously and cook over a low heat until the beans are soft, about 1½ hours. Drain and set aside.

Heat the olive oil in a separate cooking pot (large enough to hold all the ingredients comfortably) over a low heat. Add the onions, dried chilli and a pinch of salt. Sweat gently until the onions are soft and translucent.

Now add the celery, carrots, garlic, sage, potatoes and farro. Cook for a couple of minutes to allow the heat to begin to release the flavours of the vegetables, then add the tomatoes. Cover and simmer over a low heat for 20 minutes.

Stir in the cooked beans, then cover with about 1 litre water – just enough for a thick brothy base in which the vegetables can cook properly. Add the cavolo nero and reduce the heat to low. Cover and cook for a further hour until the vegetables are really soft. Add a generous pinch of salt and a few good grindings of black pepper.

Remove from the heat and allow to cool completely. Let the ribollita stand for a couple of hours – this will improve the flavour no end!

To serve, reheat the soup. Taste and adjust the seasoning if necessary, then drizzle generously with extra virgin olive oil. Turn up the heat to emulsify, then ladle into warm bowls.

Slow-cooked dishes more often than not taste better if they are removed from the stove once they are cooked and allowed to settle to room temperature, then reheated to serve. Also, these dishes call for patience from the start. Slow, gentle cooking of onions, chilli, garlic or whatever else the recipe asks you to lay down will give a much better flavour than if you rush it. Gentle, respectful cooking results in a dish that is sweeter, richer and far more complex...

Wild sea bass with salmoriglio

Salmoriglio is a pungent marinade-come-sauce from Sicily. It is traditionally made with oregano though I generally use marjoram, as we have a profusion in our vegetable garden during the summer. You can make the sauce a few days in advance – leaving the flavours to mature and intensify at room temperature (not in the fridge) – but add the lemon juice just before you are ready to use it. In the summer, I often serve this fish dish simply with sliced perfectly ripe tomatoes, drizzled with olive oil, and really good, chewy peasant-style bread.

Serves 4

4 wild sea bass fillets (with skin), about 180g each

1 tbsp olive oil

sea salt and freshly ground black pepper

lemon wedges, to serve

Salmoriglio

4 small garlic cloves, peeled and roughly sliced

1/2 tsp good-quality sea salt

1/2 tsp dried red chilli flakes

bunch of marjoram or oregano, leaves only

220ml extra virgin olive oil (I use a light, fruity Sicilian oil)

1/2 lemon

First make the salmoriglio. Pound the garlic using a pestle and mortar to a rough paste, then add the salt and continue to pound until smooth. Add the chilli and marjoram and pound lightly, then pour in the olive oil and stir well to combine. If using straight away squeeze over the lemon juice; otherwise set aside, adding the lemon juice just before serving.

To cook the fish, preheat the grill. On the skin side only, brush with olive oil and season generously with salt and pepper. Lay the fish, flesh side down, on the grill rack and place under the heat.

Cook the sea bass fillets without turning for 5–6 minutes or until the skin is blistered and deliciously crisp, and the flesh underneath is delicately translucent.

Carefully transfer the fish fillets, skin side up, to warm plates and spoon over the salmoriglio. Serve at once, with lemon wedges, good bread or new potatoes and a salad.

Salmoriglio is an excellent marinade for chicken or lamb, and is perfect for basting fish and red meat during cooking. Or you can simply spoon it over cooked fish (as here), meat or vegetables before serving. It is particularly good smeared over grilled aubergines or roasted squash, or drizzled over ripe tomatoes.

Leaves

I have often thought that my very last meal on this earth would have to be some sort of salad. Other things would certainly be involved, but it would be composed primarily of leaves, dressed with a beautiful extra virgin olive oil and a touch of acidity. I eat salad every day – I never tire of it as I find the possible flavour combinations endless.

When I grew up in Australia the choice of salad leaves was limited – to crunchy, watery Iceberg, crisp Cos and a few other lettuces, but little else. Rocket, radicchio, mâche and frisée were unheard of, and it wasn't until I moved to Europe in my early twenties that I was able to sample all the beautiful loose-leafed and tightly spun varieties from France, Italy and elsewhere. I love them all, but rocket, purslane and baby spinach (or pousse) feature strongly in my dishes. And my favourite family of leaves encompasses tardivo, treviso, Castelfranco and pissenlit (or dandelion), all of which are elegant to behold and bittersweet to taste.

Almost everything I serve at the restaurant or at home arrives with a tangle of one leaf or another. Sometimes, when the leaves are perfect, I'll present just one variety on its own – choosing it carefully to complement the food it is to be served with. At other times a variety of leaves is called for – some sweet, some bitter, some with bite, some soft – often with a handful of herb leaves thrown in.

◊

We grow lots of young, sweet leaves in the summer, including purslane, bull's blood, lollo rosso, mizuna, mignonette, pea shoots and rocket, which has a strength of flavour that I love. Rocket thrives easily, and with each cutting, it grows back stronger – and seemingly more intensely flavoured. I urge you to try and grow some, even if you only have a tub or window box. I'm also very fond of purslane – both the summer and winter varieties. Succulent and bouncy, it adds a fresh clean bite to salads. Pea shoots lend a similar vibrancy – totally delicious, they taste more of sweet fresh peas than the vegetables do themselves.

Some of the most interesting leaves, including the endives, red-leafed chicories (tardivo, treviso and radicchio), Castelfranco (illustrated on pages 84–5) and pissenlit or dandelion (shown left) are winter leaves. Some are attractively speckled, others striped, but all have a languid beauty that is truly breathtaking. Their distinctive bitter taste counterbalances rich winter dishes perfectly.

◊

All things must be considered when composing a salad – texture and flavour of course, but also the colour and shape of the various leaves.

Do try to grow some of your own leaves, or at least source more exciting varieties from farmers' markets and good greengrocers. Obviously, all leaves are best used as soon as possible after picking or buying. If you need to store them for a day or two, keep them loosely covered with a damp tea towel in the salad drawer of the fridge, but handle carefully, for they are fragile and suffer fridge burn and bruising easily.

Wash salad leaves gently and only if they really need it. Gently pat them dry with a clean tea towel or invest in a good salad spinner. This is essential, for leaves that are water sodden will be heavy and disappointing – and the dressing will taste diluted and slip from the leaves rather than cling to them.

◊

Like all things, leaves have their season and none is available all year round. The winter months are filled with the bitter leaves, whereas in summer we have the softer fresher varieties. There is, however, something to enjoy every month throughout the year.

Middle Eastern salad of cucumber, lettuce and herbs

I love the idea of this salad. When I was a child, my father, who rarely ever cooked, would sometimes prepare a chopped salad that he had eaten in America. It comprised several ingredients – often crunchy lettuce, sweet tomatoes and cheese or some form of meat – chopped into small pieces and tossed with a good dressing. This is more a Middle East version, without meat or cheese. It is almost the consistency of gazpacho, but laced with plenty of cool, crunchy Cos lettuce.

Serves 4

2 very ripe tomatoes

1 small cucumber

1 red onion, peeled and finely chopped

1 red pepper, cored, deseeded and chopped

6 radishes, chopped

1 red chilli, deseeded and very finely chopped

bunch of flat leaf parsley, leaves only, chopped

bunch of mint, leaves only, chopped

small bunch of dill, leaves only, finely chopped

1/2 tsp dried mint

1 tsp red wine vinegar

juice of 1/2 lemon

1/2 tsp pomegranate molasses

sea salt

3 tbsp extra virgin olive oil

1 pomegranate

1 small, tender Cos lettuce

Chop the tomatoes into small dice and place in a large bowl. Halve the cucumber lengthways and scoop out the seeds, then cut into pieces the same size as the tomatoes and add to the bowl. Add the red onion, red pepper, radishes, chilli, chopped fresh herbs and dried mint. Stir well to combine.

In a separate bowl, combine the red wine vinegar, lemon juice, pomegranate molasses, a good pinch of salt and the extra virgin olive oil. Stir well and pour over the chopped vegetables. Toss gently and leave to macerate for 10 minutes.

Hold the pomegranate in one hand and gently tap it all over with a rolling pin to loosen the seeds. Now cut the fruit in half and extract the seeds with your fingers – do this over a bowl to catch them and any juice. Pick out any strands of bitter pith that have dropped into the bowl.

Just before serving, shred the lettuce and toss through the salad. Taste and season with a little more salt if necessary. Pile onto a serving plate and sprinkle with the pomegranate seeds. Serve with warm flat bread, or as an accompaniment to simply grilled fish.

Pink grapefruit, avocado and watercress salad

This elegant, light salad is ideal to serve as a first course. Pink grapefruit and peppery watercress cut the richness of avocado, and a scattering of toasted hazelnuts and hazelnut oil in the dressing suggest a flavour of early autumn. Parma ham is a graceful inclusion, but you can leave it out for a lighter vegetarian salad if you like.

Serves 4

16 shelled hazelnuts

bunch of watercress

1 pink grapefruit

1 ripe avocado

8–12 slices of Parma ham

8–12 wafer-thin slices of young pecorino (optional)

1 tbsp finely chopped parsley

Dressing

1 tbsp Dijon mustard

2 tbsp sherry vinegar

sea salt and freshly ground black pepper

40ml mild-tasting extra virgin olive oil

3 tbsp hazelnut oil

First make the dressing. Combine the mustard and sherry vinegar in a bowl and add a pinch each of salt and pepper. Whisk in the olive oil, followed by the hazelnut oil to emulsify, then set aside.

Preheat the oven to 180°C/Gas 4. Place the nuts on a baking tray and roast in the middle of the oven for 3–4 minutes to warm and release their flavour. Turn into a cloth and rub gently to remove the skins, then roughly chop the nuts.

For the salad, wash the watercress and gently pat dry. Peel the grapefruit, removing all the pith, then cut out the segments over a large bowl to catch the juice as well as the segments. Halve, stone and peel the avocado, then cut into slices, similar in size to the grapefruit. Add to the grapefruit with the watercress and toss gently with your fingers to mix.

If the dressing has separated on standing, give it a whisk, then drizzle half of it over the salad and toss lightly, so you don't break up the avocado or grapefruit. Taste and adjust the seasoning.

Arrange the salad on a plate, interleaving the Parma ham slices and pecorino if using, with the watercress, grapefruit and avocado. Sprinkle with the chopped parsley and drizzle over the remaining dressing. Finally, scatter over the hazelnuts and serve.

Roasted vegetable salad with rocket and tomatoes

Deeply colourful, sweet and warm, this is a favourite salad of mine. We make it with rocket and beetroot from our garden – I also like to throw in the beetroot tops, which make the most delicious salad leaf. Don't drown this beautiful salad with dressing … you want to allow all the colours and earthy sweet flavours to shine through.

Serves 4

12 small young beetroot, with leafy tops

1 small red onion, peeled and sliced into pinwheels

4 tbsp olive oil

sea salt and freshly ground black pepper

1 tbsp balsamic vinegar

1 large (or 2 medium) sweet potato

1/2 tbsp maple syrup

1/2 tbsp tamari or soy sauce

1 dried red chilli, crumbled

1/2 lime

2 small fennel bulbs, trimmed

12 little ripe tomatoes, such as San Marzano, datterini or cherry tomatoes

large handful of rocket leaves

extra virgin olive oil, to drizzle

Dressing

180ml thick Greek-style yoghurt

10 drops of Tabasco

juice of 1/2 lime

40ml extra virgin olive oil

small bunch of coriander, leaves only

First make the dressing. Put the yoghurt in a bowl and stir in the Tabasco, most of the lime juice, the olive oil and a pinch of salt. Chop the coriander finely and stir into the dressing. Taste and add a little more salt or lime juice if needed. Set aside.

Preheat the oven to 200°C/Gas 6. Scrub the beetroot well under cold running water to remove any dirt, but don't bother to peel them. Cut off the tops, wash these, pat them dry and set aside for later.

Put the beetroot and onion rings in a roasting tray, pour over 2 tbsp olive oil and season with salt and pepper. Cover tightly with foil and roast in the oven for 40 minutes or until the beetroot is tender when pierced with a sharp knife. Take out the onion rings and set aside. Return the beetroot to the oven and bake, uncovered, for a further 15 minutes until the skins are crinkly. Place in a bowl and dress while warm with the balsamic vinegar. Set aside to cool.

Meanwhile, peel the sweet potato and cut into 4cm chunks. Place in a bowl and spoon over the maple syrup, tamari or soy and 1 tbsp olive oil. Toss to coat, then place in a roasting tray and scatter over the chilli. Roast, uncovered, on the middle shelf of the oven for 35 minutes or until tender when pierced with a knife. Remove and while warm, squeeze over the lime juice. Set aside to cool.

Quarter the fennel bulbs and place in a roasting tray. Season with salt and pepper and drizzle with 1 tbsp olive oil. Cover with foil and bake in the oven for 20 minutes, then remove the foil and throw in the little tomatoes. Return to the oven and cook, uncovered, for a further 15–20 minutes or until the fennel is soft and the tomatoes are soft and oozing their juice. Remove and allow to cool.

Put the rocket and beetroot tops in a bowl, dress with a little extra virgin olive oil and season lightly. Arrange the salad on individual plates, layering the leaves and roasted vegetables, and spooning over a little dressing here and there as you go. Serve at once.

Salad of summer leaves and flowers

When combining different leaves to make a salad, it is important to
consider flavour, but also texture and colour. I like to include bitter
as well as sweet leaves, choosing some that are watery and crunchy,
others that are soft and succulent. A peppery note, of watercress or
rocket, is a good addition, too. Among my other favourites are baby
spinach and chard, purslane, bull's blood, pea shoots, Cos, escarole,
mâche and the slightly bitter members of the *chicoria* family.
Sometimes we add flowers to our salads, which not only look
beautiful, they also have their own distinctive flavours. My
preferred dressing for leaves is simply olive oil and lemon juice.

Serves 4

selection of different leaves
(see above)

handful of soft herb leaves
(chervil, flat leaf parsley,
basil etc.)

handful of edible flowers
(nasturtiums, violets, pansies,
borage and/or other herb
flowers), optional

Dressing

juice of 1/2 lemon, or to taste

100ml mild-tasting extra virgin
olive oil

sea salt and freshly ground
black pepper

For the dressing, whisk the lemon juice and extra virgin olive oil
together to combine, seasoning with salt and pepper to taste.
Seasoning is very important – salt really makes leaves come alive.

If necessary, wash the salad and herb leaves and gently pat dry.
Place in a large bowl and toss with a little of the dressing. Scatter
over the flowers if using, to serve.

Keep any leftover dressing in a screw-topped jar and use within a
day or two, shaking it well to re-emulsify.

Always dress leaves using your fingertips – a light
touch is imperative – but you also need to be quite thorough.
An underdressed salad is very disappointing to eat. Equally
don't overdo it, as too much oil or vinaigrette will overpower
the delicate flavours of the leaves.

Langoustines with cooked spinach, purple basil and tomato aïoli

I love this combination of earthy, inky green leaves and sweet, succulent langoustines – or Dublin Bay prawns as they are also known. The tomato aïoli brings the flavours together perfectly. If you cannot get langoustines, you'll find the dish also works beautifully with prawns or griddled scallops.

Serves 4

about 24 live langoustines (6 per person)

sea salt and freshly ground black pepper

40ml extra virgin olive oil

grated zest of 1 lemon

juice of 1/2 lemon

300g young spinach leaves (or pousse)

bunch of purple basil, leaves only

Fresh tomato aïoli

3 little ripe plum tomatoes

3 organic free-range egg yolks

1/2 tsp Dijon mustard

2 garlic cloves, peeled and crushed

juice of 1 lemon

250ml extra virgin olive oil

Ask your fishmonger for live langoustines and keep them in a box covered with damp newspaper until ready to cook.

Start by making the aïoli. Preheat the oven to 200°C/Gas 6. Pierce each tomato once with a small sharp knife and place in a small roasting tray. Roast on the middle shelf of the oven for 15 minutes or until the tomatoes are soft and their skins have split slightly. Set aside to cool.

Place the egg yolks in a food processor and add the mustard, garlic, lemon juice and the cooled tomatoes. Add a pinch of salt and a little pepper. Whiz briefly to combine. Now, with the motor running, slowly add the olive oil through the feeder tube in a fine stream until it is all incorporated and the aïoli is emulsified. Taste and adjust the seasoning.

For the langoustines, place a large pot of water on to boil and salt it generously. When it reaches a rolling boil, drop in the langoustines and cook for 3 minutes. Remove and allow to cool. When cool enough to handle, peel the langoustines, removing the flesh in one piece. Season with salt and pepper and dress with a little of the olive oil. Sprinkle with a few drops of lemon juice.

Wash the spinach in several changes of cold water to ensure that no dirt is clinging to the leaves. Warm a medium heavy-based saucepan over a medium heat. Add the spinach, in batches if necessary, with just the water clinging to the leaves. This alone will create steam and allow the spinach to quickly wilt. Once wilted, tip it into a colander and allow to cool. When cool, squeeze the spinach between the palms of your hands to remove as much moisture as possible. Dress with the remaining olive oil, and the lemon zest and juice. Season with salt and pepper.

To assemble the salad, place the spinach in a bowl with the basil and langoustines. Toss together gently to combine. Arrange on individual serving plates and spoon a little of the aïoli over the top.

Salad of poached salmon, black rice and watercress

For the best possible flavour, you would need to poach a whole salmon, but given the size this is often impractical – you'll most probably find it more convenient to poach fillets. Choose wild salmon though, as the flavour is far superior and more delicate. Watercress is a natural partner for salmon, as its slightly peppery leaves balance the sweet flavour of the flesh. If black rice is difficult to locate, you'll find cooked cannellini beans are equally delicious.

Serves 6

1kg wild salmon (see above)

2 carrots, peeled and chopped

2 celery sticks, chopped

small bunch of tarragon

3 bay leaves

6 black peppercorns

70g black rice (venero nero)

salt and freshly ground black pepper

4 tbsp extra virgin olive oil

juice of 1 lime

bunch of watercress

Dressing

2 ripe tomatoes, chopped

1 tbsp freshly grated horseradish

finely grated zest and juice of 1 lime

2 tbsp olive oil

120ml crème fraîche

To finish

small handful of chervil leaves, finely chopped

Place the salmon in a wide, shallow pan with the carrots, celery, tarragon, bay leaves and peppercorns. Pour over sufficient water to cover and bring to a bare simmer over a medium heat. As soon as the water reaches a simmer, turn off the heat and let the sh cook in the residual heat of the poaching liquor as it cools.

Cook the black rice in boiling salted water according to the packet instructions until al dente; it will take about 35–40 minutes.

Mix 2 tbsp olive oil with the lime juice and some salt and pepper. When the salmon is cool, remove it from the liquor to a plate and brush with the lime and oil mixture. Set aside.

To make the dressing, put the chopped tomatoes into a bowl and stir in the horseradish, lime zest and juice, olive oil and crème fraîche. Season with a good pinch of salt.

To assemble the salad, wash the watercress and pat dry, then place in a bowl and dress with 1 tbsp olive oil and a small pinch of salt. Dress the rice in a separate bowl, also with 1 tbsp olive oil and a little salt. Remove the skin from the salmon and gently flake into pieces, using your fingers.

Arrange the watercress, rice and salmon on individual plates, layering them attractively. Drizzle over the dressing and sprinkle with the chervil to serve.

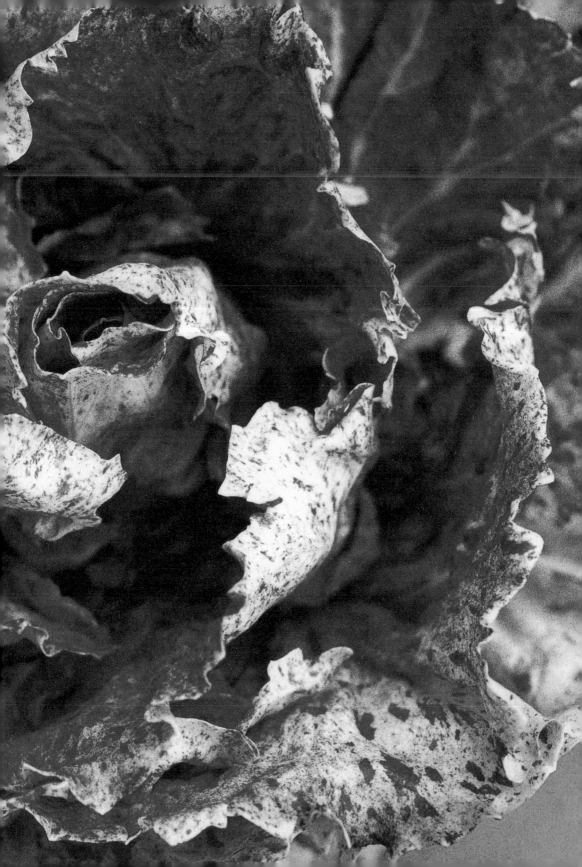

Citrus

When I started following the rhythm of the seasons in my cooking, I remember being so surprised to learn that citrus were primarily winter fruits. To me, they speak so absolutely of summer, of sunshine and warmth. Their powerful burst of flavour suggests a product of blue skies, long days and, most importantly, heat. Now I realise that nature's majesty has bestowed these jewels during the winter months to give a sense of sustenance and hope, such is the perfection of the natural world.

Intense and beautiful in colour, with clear, clean, top note flavours, they are a real gift and offer such diversity. Tarocco blood oranges, Seville oranges, kumquats, clementines, mandarins, pink grapefruit, cedros (citrons), lemons and limes are among the citrus fruit that I love to cook with. In truth, I would find it almost impossible to work without citrus fruits – their flavours are as necessary to my cooking as the use of salt.

Many citrus trees can, in fact, bear fruit for most of the year, though they blossom and fruit most notably in late December and January. Some not-to-be-missed varieties, however – including clementines, Seville oranges, mandarins and blood oranges – have a short season, lasting only two or three months during the winter or spring. Most of our citrus fruit comes from Italy, Spain and North Africa, though at Petersham we are fortunate to have a number of trees, including lemon, kaffir lime, Meyer lemon and kumquat. To be able to walk into a greenhouse and pluck lemons and other citrus fruit from the tree through the year is a real treat, not least because the trees themselves are visually so beautiful.

◊

When you are buying citrus fruit, choose fruit that feels heavy for its size. Avoid any with bruises, but don't worry about blemishes, as these occur naturally during ripening. To give it a longer shelf life, most citrus fruit is waxed, which is annoying. Buy unwaxed fruit if you possibly can, especially if you are using the zest or peel (all organic fruit is unwaxed). Otherwise scrub the fruit well before use.

◊

Lemon juice is the ingredient, along with salt, that I depend on more than anything in the kitchen. It makes food come alive and I use the sharp juice to flavour so many dishes. Never is there a day when my kitchen is without a bowl of lemons.

All citrus fruits have intensely flavoured zest and juice, which give a zing to dishes – sweet and savoury. I use freshly squeezed lemon juice in so many ways – to make lemonade; dress vegetables and salads; drizzle over fish; cut the richness of mayonnaise made with extra virgin olive oil, and so on. The peel I add to slow-cooked dishes to impart vibrancy and life, and I strew the grated zest on almost everything – to add freshness and high notes.

Blood oranges, at their peak in January and February, are one of my favourites. I use them to make jellies and other palate-cleansing desserts. Their juice also lends a vibrancy to savoury dishes – try it in an aïoli to serve with roasted sea bass or deep-fried artichokes. Warm and intense, this garlicky mayonnaise with a hint of citrus is a beautiful pale orangey-red colour.

In January, we make big vats of marmalade from the bitter juice and skin of Seville oranges to sell in the shop at Petersham; we also eat it on sourdough toast cooked over the grill to take the chill off the early mornings.

We pickle limes to make a sour relish, which is perfect with dishes that are spice laden and Indian in spirit. We also preserve lemons in salt – to chop and add to veal stews, or slow-cooked dishes that are Middle Eastern in feel. Their peculiar and pungent taste is unique.

And we candy everything we possibly can, especially cedro (citron) peel and pinwheels of clementines and blood oranges. To my mind, nothing works better with bitter chocolate than candied orange peel.

Lemonade

Week in, week out, we make this mouth-wateringly sharp, refreshing drink – just as we did when the restaurant first opened without a licence to sell alcohol. When I see a full jug of freshly made lemonade, crammed with crushed ice and fresh mint, it still makes me smile. It reflects most truly our roots and our ethos...

Makes about 2 litres

8 lemons

200g caster sugar

about 1.5–2 litres sparkling (or plain) water, to dilute

mint sprigs, to serve

Squeeze the juice from the lemons and pour into a saucepan. Add the sugar and stir well. Place over a medium heat and bring to a simmer, stirring every now and then to dissolve the sugar. Cook gently for 5–6 minutes, then remove from the heat. Pour into a jug and allow to cool.

When completely cool, cover and place in the fridge. This lemonade base keeps well, though you'll probably use it all within a few days.

To serve, pour some lemonade base into a jug – to fill it by about a quarter. Add plenty of ice and top up with sparkling water to taste. Add a handful of mint sprigs and serve.

Lemon and orange curd

Sharp, yet sweet and comforting, this is a really satisfying thing to make. Old-fashioned in a way, it has a deep, nostalgic flavour, triggering memories – flavours that achieve this are particularly special to me. You can vary the taste by adding the juice of other citrus fruit, like blood oranges, as I have here. But don't be tempted to omit the lemon altogether as its acidity is needed to prevent the curd from becoming overly sweet.

Makes about 500g

finely grated zest and juice of 2 unwaxed lemons

finely grated zest and juice of 1 blood orange

140g caster sugar

6 egg yolks

180g unsalted butter, cut into small pieces

Mix the lemon and orange zest and juice, sugar and egg yolks together in a heatproof bowl until well combined. Stand the bowl over a pan of simmering water (or simply pour the mixture straight into a medium heavy-based saucepan and place over a very low heat if you are confident that you can keep the direct heat low enough).

Stir continuously with a wooden spoon as the mixture begins to warm and gradually thicken. Don't allow it to boil or it will curdle. Once the curd is thick enough to coat the back of the spoon, about 7–10 minutes, remove from the heat.

Immediately stir in the butter, cube by cube. Strain the curd through a fine sieve into a clean bowl or a warm sterilised jar. Cover or seal and store in the fridge. It will keep for a good week or so.

Deep-fried artichokes and lemon with mint and anchovy dressing

I like to deep-fry things in the manner of Italian *fritto misto* – it is a lovely informal way of mixing and matching ingredients. Over the years I have deep-fried almost everything, from little anchovies to soft ripe figs! A good accompanying sauce is essential. This sharp, salty dressing is a perfect foil for crispy battered artichokes – try serving it with other deep-fried vegetables too.

Serves 4

12 small, tender artichokes

juice of 1 lemon (if preparing ahead)

2 unwaxed lemons

corn oil, for deep-frying

Batter

375g plain flour

pinch of sea salt

125ml olive oil

80ml sparkling water

1 egg white

Anchovy and mint dressing

5 good-quality anchovy fillets, packed in salt or olive oil

bunch of mint, leaves only

2–2 1/2 tbsp red wine vinegar

120ml extra virgin olive oil

You'll have more batter than you need here, but it keeps well in the fridge and is perfect for a *piccolo fritto* of lovage leaves. Simply draw the leaves through the batter and deep-fry until crisp and golden. Use as a garnish for meat or fish.

First make the batter. Sift the flour into a bowl, add a pinch of salt and make a well in the middle. Pour in the olive oil, whisking well to combine, then whisk in the sparkling water. In another bowl, whisk the egg white to firm peaks, then fold into the batter. (You can make this batter a few hours ahead.)

For the dressing, rinse the anchovies well if they are packed in salt, then drain and pat dry. Place the anchovies in a blender, along with the mint leaves and 2 tbsp wine vinegar. With the motor running, slowly pour in the olive oil through the feeder tube until it is all incorporated. Taste and add a little more wine vinegar if you like; you shouldn't need any salt.

To prepare the artichokes, trim away the darker tough outer leaves with a sharp knife and trim and peel the stem. Cut off the tops of the artichoke leaves at the point where their colour becomes darker. Now cut each artichoke in half lengthways and remove the hairy choke. If not using immediately, immerse in a bowl of water acidulated with the lemon juice to prevent them from discolouring. Slice the lemons into fairly thinly rounds (but not so thin that they will fall apart when deep-fried).

When ready to cook, drain the artichokes and pat dry. Heat the corn oil in a deep-fryer or other suitable heavy-based pan to 180°C, or until a cube of bread dropped in sizzles and browns quickly. You'll need to cook the artichokes in batches. Dip in the batter and turn to coat, then lift out letting the excess batter fall off. Deep-fry three or four at a time for about 1 1/2 minutes until golden and tender. Remove and drain on kitchen paper; keep hot while you cook the rest. Deep-fry the lemon slices in the same way – don't overcrowd the pan or they will stick together. When golden, remove and drain.

Serve the crispy artichokes and lemon slices on warm plates drizzled with the anchovy and mint dressing. I like to serve a simply dressed rocket salad alongside, for a nice clean contrast.

Grilled poussins with lemon, marjoram, flat bread and garlicky yoghurt

We cooked this in a wood-fired oven one beautiful, warm summer's evening. The combination of tender chicken, garlicky yoghurt and sweet summer tomatoes – mopped up with the thinnest possible bread – was truly memorable. It helped that the poussins were salted beforehand, which makes their flesh really tender and flavourful. You might not be able to create quite the same effect without a wood-fired oven, but it will taste delicious all the same…

Serves 4

4 poussins, spatchcocked

1 tbsp coarse sea salt

juice of 1 lemon

small bunch of marjoram, leaves only, chopped

1 red chilli, finely sliced

4 tbsp extra virgin olive oil

Yoghurt dressing

300ml thick Greek style-yoghurt

2 garlic cloves, peeled and crushed

pinch of sea salt

40ml extra virgin olive oil

To serve

4 Arab-style flat breads or pitta breads

about 12 cherry tomatoes, halved

large handful of wild rocket

few marjoram leaves, roughly torn

A day ahead, lay the spatchcocked poussins on a board and sprinkle evenly all over with the coarse salt. Cover with a clean cloth and place in the fridge.

The next day, an hour or so before you will be ready to cook, take the poussins out of the fridge and allow them to return to room temperature. Brush off any excess salt and do not re-season. Sprinkle with the lemon juice. Stir the marjoram and chilli into the olive oil, then rub this mixture all over both the birds and set aside.

To make the yoghurt dressing, put the yoghurt into a bowl and add the garlic, salt and olive oil. Stir well, then taste and adjust the seasoning if necessary.

When ready to cook, heat up your grill or barbecue. When it is really hot, lay the poussins skin side down on the grill rack and cook for 6–8 minutes. Then turn and grill for a further 8 minutes on the other side. The skin should be golden and blistered in some places, the flesh underneath meltingly tender. A minute or two before the poussins will be ready, add the flat breads to the grill to warm through, turning once.

Arrange the poussins on warm plates, with the warm breads, tomatoes and rocket. Spoon over the yoghurt dressing and scatter over a little marjoram to serve.

Clementines with Medjool dates, pomegranates and honeyed almonds

This is a very simple fruity winter dessert, based on a handful of ingredients that are in season, at their best and go together beautifully. Like all simple things, it relies on good produce, prepared thoughtfully and as close to eating as is possible. I use the majestic Medjool dates, which lend a lovely caramely taste. And the honey I like to use is chestnut – dark in colour, with a slightly bitter, molasses flavour.

Serves 4

80ml chestnut honey (or other fragrant honey)

20 blanched almonds

1 pomegranate

4 clementines

6 Medjool dates

4 rounded tbsp mascarpone

Put the honey into a saucepan and bring to a simmer over a medium heat. Add the almonds and stir once or twice to coat them in the honey. Cook for a couple of minutes, then remove from the heat and set aside.

Now you need to extract the seeds from the pomegranate. I find the easiest way to do this is by holding the pomegranate in one hand and gently tapping it all over with a wooden rolling pin, moving the pomegranate as I tap it. This loosens the teardrop-shaped seeds from the bitter white pith that clings to them. Cut the fruit in half – the seeds should now be easy for you to remove with your fingers. Do this over a bowl, to catch any juice. When you've finished, pick out any strands of bitter membrane that might have dropped into the bowl.

Using a small sharp knife, slice off both ends of the clementines, then cut away the peel and pith, following the contour of the fruit. Now cut the segments free, catching the juice and adding it to the pomegranate seeds as you do so. Cut each date into 5 or 6 slices, discarding the seeds.

To assemble, arrange the clementine segments on large individual plates. Scatter over the dates, pomegranate seeds and juice, placing a spoonful of mascarpone in the centre. Scatter over the honeyed almonds and serve.

Blood oranges with warm honey and rosemary

This is one of my all-time favourite desserts. I love its utter simplicity and purity of flavour. It is the perfect way to round off one of those slow-cooked slightly heavier meals that we are drawn to during the colder months. As a soaring clean, clear palate-cleanser, it leaves you feeling lighter and refreshed at the end.

Serves 4

6 blood oranges

130ml light, fragrant honey, such as acacia

3 tbsp water

3–4 rosemary stems, plus extra sprigs to finish

1 small dried red chilli, deseeded and very finely sliced (optional)

To prepare the oranges, using a small sharp knife, slice off both ends, then stand upright on a board. Running the knife from the top to the bottom, cut away the peel and pith, following the contour of the fruit. Now slice the oranges across into pinwheels – I usually get 5 slices from each orange. Set aside while you warm the honey.

Put the honey and water into a small saucepan. Lay the rosemary on a wooden chopping board and using a rolling pin, gently pound the stalk and leaves to bruise them and release their flavour. Add the rosemary to the pan and place over a very low heat. Allow the honey to warm through very gently for a few minutes, stirring from time to time; don't let the mixture boil. Take off the heat and set aside to infuse for 10 minutes, then take out the rosemary.

To serve, arrange the orange pinwheels on individual plates. Sprinkle with the dried chilli if using, and spoon over the infused honey. Scatter over a few fresh rosemary sprigs and serve.

Pink grapefruit and sherry sherbet

This icy-cold dessert is so light it is almost ethereal. The addition of Pedro Ximénez, a dark, rich raisin-flavoured sweet sherry, underpins the sherbet. You can use blood orange, clementine or mandarin juice rather than pink grapefruit if you prefer – all of these have distinctive flavours and work well here. You'll need approximately 600ml juice.

Serves 4

6 pink grapefruit

150g caster sugar

180ml double cream

1 vanilla pod, split lengthways

3 tbsp Pedro Ximénez sherry

Cut the pink grapefruit in half and squeeze to extract as much juice from them as possible. Strain the juice through a colander into a bowl and set aside.

Put the sugar and cream into a small heavy-based saucepan. Scrape the seeds from the vanilla pod and add them to the pan together with the empty pod. Place over a medium heat and bring just to the boil, stirring once or twice to dissolve the sugar. Lower the heat and simmer gently for a minute or so – you simply want to infuse the cream with the flavour of vanilla. Remove and set aside to cool.

Once the infused cream is cool, pour it through a sieve onto the grapefruit juice and stir well, then add the sherry. Pour the mixture into an ice-cream maker and churn until thickened, following the manufacturer's instructions.

Spoon into chilled bowls and serve the sherbet just as it is, to fully appreciate its refreshing taste and wonderful texture.

Ices and sorbets need to have a strong, distinguishing taste before they are frozen. Chilling dulls flavour, so they will taste more subtle once frozen.

Chocolate-dipped candied cedro and clementines

As a child, candied orange peel dipped in chocolate was one of my favourite things. My mother would serve these bittersweet treats with coffee at the end of a dinner party and I thought they were the most glamorous things in the world! I still love the taste. We make these around Christmas time to serve with coffee in the restaurant. The candied fruit, before dipping, can be wrapped and kept in the fridge for 4 months to chop and use in pastries and desserts.

Serves 8–10

2 cedros (or citrons), well washed

4 clementines, well washed

1kg caster sugar

1 litre water

250g good-quality dark chocolate (minimum 64% cocoa solids)

Cut the cedros in half straight through the centre. Scrape out and discard the small central area of flesh. Now slice each cedro half into 5 slices. Do this with the second fruit – giving you 20 slices altogether. Slice the clementines into rounds, leaving on the skin.

Place all the fruit in a large saucepan and cover with cold water. Bring to the boil over a low heat and simmer for 10 minutes, then drain. Repeat this process twice more – so that the fruit has been blanched and drained 3 times.

Return the fruit to the saucepan and add the sugar and water. Stir carefully over a low heat until the sugar has dissolved. Continue to cook the fruit very gently until it becomes translucent; this will take about 30 minutes. Turn off the heat and leave the fruit to cool slowly in the sugar syrup for 30 minutes or so.

Drain the fruit and arrange the pieces on a wire rack over a tray (as shown on the previous page) or on a sheet of non-stick baking parchment, making sure that they are not touching each other. Allow to dry, uncovered, overnight.

The next day, break up the chocolate into a heatproof bowl and set over a pan of gently simmering water (making sure the water is not in contact with the bowl). Leave to melt gently, without stirring. Remove the bowl from the heat. Dip the candied clementine wheels into the chocolate one by one to half-coat them, then lay on greaseproof paper to dry. Do the same with the cedro. Once set, store in an airtight container and refrigerate. Use within a few days.

Cedros (or citrons) look like large knobbly lemons. They have very little actual flesh, but are prized for their pith. This is thick, creamy and much less bitter than the pith of lemons or oranges – making it perfect to candy.

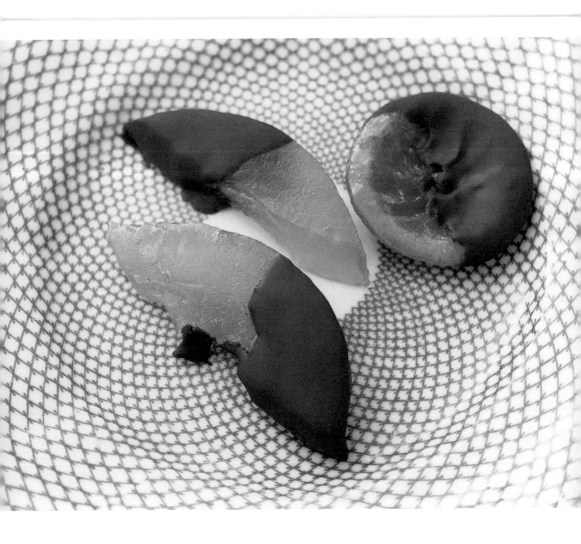

Pulses & grains

Pulses and grains are probably the mainstay of my cooking, appearing in different guises on the restaurant menu, but also in my cooking at home. They are primarily the foods that my children have grown up on – and what I crave to eat myself. Inexpensive and nutritious, it is no wonder that they feature so prominently in peasant cooking. They also transgress the seasons, as you can enjoy fresh pulses during the summer months and the more familiar dried pulses from autumn through winter and spring.

Cooked with sympathetic flavourings, pulses and grains taste not only delicious, but also good for you, which they are. This is my favourite kind of food… when I eat, I like to feel that my body is benefiting from what I am putting into it. That is not to say that I am preoccupied with health in any way – health fads are strange to me and dull food is inexcusable to my mind. I want to eat food that is satisfying and full of flavour, and this is what I endeavour to cook.

We grow borlotti beans

in our vegetable garden. They climb on willow cages skilfully constructed by Lucy, our gardener every couple of years. Magenta and cream in colour, these elegant beans are one of nature's wonders as their colours are reversed inside the pods. Strangely, once cooked, they turn a dull mousey brown, but what they lose in beauty they more than make up for in flavour.

Among my favourite pulses and grains are beautiful borlotti beans, cannellini beans, little lentils from Puy or Umbria, arrocina – a lovely little white bean from Spain, farro from Italy and coco beans, which I've only ever encountered fresh during the summer. We pod fresh pulses and cook them briefly until tender during the summer months. In winter we soak dried beans overnight and braise them slowly and gently to serve with slow-cooked lamb or beef, or to add in moderation to seafood stews. It is important not to overdo it though, or you'll make the dish feel heavy.

◊

Dried pulses are available all year round, but ideally you want to be cooking last year's harvest. Buy from speciality shops, such as Middle Eastern or Italian or Greek, where you think the turnover is likely to be high and therefore the produce fresh.

Ideally dried beans should always be soaked overnight, then drained and cooked with herbs, garlic, perhaps a tomato or two and a dried chilli. Never add salt until they begin to soften, as it toughens the skins. If, like me, remembering to pre-soak pulses is beyond your usual level of organisation, there is a way round… Rinse the beans, place them in a pan and cover with cold water, then bring to the boil. Drain, return to the pan and cover a second time with cold water flavoured with aromatics or whatever the recipe demands, then cook as if the beans have been pre-soaked.

◊

One of the things I love about pulses and grains more than anything else is their ability to absorb flavours. This is most apparent if you dress them while hot with extra virgin olive oil, a good-quality red wine vinegar or lemon juice, salt, Parmesan and herbs – sage or rosemary in the winter; basil, mint or parsley during spring and summer; marjoram, thyme or oregano in autumn. Other flavourings that go with all pulses and grains are garlic, fresh and dried chilli, ripe tomatoes, duck, red meat, fish and shellfish, cream and smoky bacon.

Farro (shown left), in particular, has an amazing ability to absorb flavours. I have fallen in love with this grain in recent years, eating it at every opportunity. One of the most ancient of all grains, it is said to have given the Roman foot soldiers the strength to conquer Europe! Known also as spelt, it is no longer fashionable except in Italy where it is used in soups, but I strongly urge you to try some…

Borlotti with garlic, sage and olive oil

We make this dish in the summer with fresh borlotti from our garden. Without doubt, these are my favourite fresh beans. Their podded beauty is mesmerising, and their flavour rich and velvety. I eat them as often at room temperature as hot – tossed through a simple salad or warm pasta. Even on toast, they are delicious.

Serves 6

1kg fresh borlotti beans, podded

1 garlic bulb, split horizontally

bunch of sage

60ml red wine vinegar

200ml extra virgin olive oil

5 good-quality anchovy fillets, packed in salt or olive oil, rinsed if salted

Preheat the oven to 200°C/Gas 6. Put the beans into a baking dish, pour over enough water to cover them comfortably, then add all the rest of the ingredients. Cover the dish tightly with foil and place on the middle shelf of the oven. Cook for 45 minutes to 1 hour or until the beans are tender to the bite.

Remove from the oven, stir well to combine and leave to cool to room temperature. The beans should be full of the flavours with which they have been cooked and allowing them to stand will enhance this further.

Eat at room temperature or reheat the beans before serving – either by themselves or as an accompaniment to slow-cooked meats or grilled fish.

In winter when fresh borlotti are not available, I make this dish with good-quality dried beans, appreciating it even more on chilly days. Use half the quantity of beans. Soak overnight, then drain and proceed as above, allowing an extra half hour or so cooking.

Chick pea and chard soup

More a meal than a soup, this is all I need to eat to pep me up at lunchtime during the week. Finished with a good splash of grassy, peppery, extra virgin olive oil, it is unctuous and truly lovely.

Serves 4

200g dried chick peas, soaked overnight

3 tbsp extra virgin olive oil, plus extra to serve

juice of 1/2 lemon

2 dried red chillies

5 garlic cloves, peeled and smashed with the back of a knife

3 rosemary sprigs

2 x 340g jars (or tinned) good-quality peeled plum tomatoes

sea salt and freshly ground black pepper

1 litre good chicken stock (or water if you prefer)

300g Swiss chard

2 slices of day-old chewy, peasant-style bread, crusts removed

75–90g Parmesan, freshly grated

Drain the chick peas, rinse and place in a large heavy-based pan. Cover generously with cold water, but do not season. Bring to the boil over a medium heat, then turn the heat down. Simmer gently for 1 1/2 hours or until the chick peas are soft, skimming away any scum from the surface every now and then. Drain and dress with 1 tbsp extra virgin olive oil and the lemon juice.

In the meantime, warm 2 tbsp extra virgin olive oil in a separate pan over a medium heat. Crumble in the chillies and add the garlic and rosemary. Cook for a minute or so to release the flavours, then add the tomatoes and stir well to break them up, adding a good pinch of salt. Cover and cook for 20 minutes, then pour in the chicken stock and cook for a further 10 minutes. finally add the cooked chick peas and simmer gently for 40 minutes.

Towards the end of the cooking time, prepare the chard. Wash and pat dry, then strip the leaves from the pale central stalk, using a small sharp knife; set aside. Trim the stalks and cut into 1cm chunks. Add these to a pan of well-salted boiling water and cook for 2 minutes, then add the soft green outer leaves and cook for a further minute. Drain.

Break the bread into small pieces and stir into the soup along with the Parmesan, turning the heat to low. Add the chard and a drizzle of extra virgin olive oil. Taste and adjust the seasoning. The soup should be deeply flavourful and thick. Add a little more Parmesan and/or olive oil if needed. Ladle into warm soup plates and serve.

Chick peas are harvested and dried at the end of the summer. Try to buy dried pulses from the new season's harvest, as these will be the sweetest and most tender of all.

Borlotti, clams and fino

The combination of fresh clams and fino sherry is a marriage made in heaven. Borlotti beans are equally at home here, as they mop up all the lovely flavours and pad the dish out. Salty, deep and delicious, I never tire of this dish.

Serves 4

1.5kg fresh clams

1 fennel bulb, trimmed and tough outer layer removed

4–5 tbsp extra virgin olive oil

1 dried red chilli

3 garlic cloves, peeled and crushed

250g good-quality peeled plum tomatoes (from a jar or tin)

sea salt and freshly ground black pepper

200ml fino sherry

400g cooked borlotti beans

bunch of flat leaf parsley, leaves stripped and roughly chopped

Pick over the clams, discarding any that are damaged or open and do not close when gently squeezed. To clean the clams, simply leave them immersed in cold water for 20 minutes or so.

Roughly chop the fennel. Heat 2 tbsp extra virgin olive oil in a heavy-based saucepan (large enough to hold all the ingredients comfortably) over a medium heat. Add the chopped fennel and cook gently for 5 minutes.

Now crumble in the chilli, and add the garlic and tomatoes. Stir well to combine and break up the tomatoes. Season with a small pinch of salt, bearing in mind the saltiness of the clams. Let bubble gently for about 10 minutes to reduce the tomatoes slightly and bring out the warmth of the chilli and flavour of the garlic.

Add the clams and sherry. Cover the pan with a tight-fitting lid, turn the heat to high and cook for about 3 minutes. Once the clams have opened, add the cooked borlotti beans and warm through.

Drizzle in the rest of the olive oil and sprinkle over the parsley. Stir well to combine and add a good grinding of pepper. Taste and adjust the seasoning if necessary – the flavour should be salty and unctuous with a marked dryness, which is the fino's contribution. Ladle into warm soup plates and serve immediately.

Clams like to feel they are still in the sea, so store them in the fridge in a covered bowl of cold water with a good pinch of salt added until you are ready to cook them.

Wild garlic and white bean curry

The beauty and subtlety of wild garlic makes this dish very appealing, and fresh curry leaves add a fragrance that is quite seductive. During the summer months we pod fresh coco beans and cook them directly in the curry until soft. In winter we soak dried cannellini beans overnight and precook them in water for an hour or so over a gentle heat, with one or two herbs added for flavour. I like to serve this curry just as it is, but you could add chunks of white fish to it.

Serves 6

400g podded fresh coco beans, or cooked dried cannellini beans (see above)

1 tsp vegetable oil

2 red onions, peeled and finely sliced

1¹/2 tsp coriander seeds

1 tsp yellow mustard seeds

1 tsp fenugreek seeds

seeds from 5 cardamom pods

3 red chillies (or more if you like heat), sliced (deseeded if you prefer less heat)

12 fresh curry leaves

6 kaffir lime leaves

small handful of coriander roots, washed and finely chopped

4 garlic cloves, peeled and crushed

2 tbsp palm sugar

juice of 2 limes

3 tbsp fish sauce

2 x 340g jars (or tinned) good-quality peeled plum tomatoes

200ml coconut milk

300g wild garlic leaves

Have the beans ready podded, or cooked if using dried beans. Heat the oil in a large heavy-based pan over a medium-low heat and sweat the onions until soft and translucent.

In a separate pan, warm all the spice seeds until they release their fragrance and just begin to jump in the pan. Tip into a mortar and grind with the pestle while still warm.

Add the warm ground spices to the softened onions along with the chillies, curry leaves, lime leaves and chopped coriander root. Cook for a further 5 minutes over a fairly low heat, then add the crushed garlic, palm sugar, lime juice and fish sauce. Stir well and cook for 5 minutes.

Add the tomatoes, stir well and cook for a further 10 minutes, then add the fresh or cooked dried beans and coconut milk. Cook gently for 10–15 minutes (or until the beans are tender if cooking fresh).

While the curry is cooking, wash the wild garlic very well, picking over each leaf thoroughly for they can carry little stones.

A couple of minutes before serving the curry, add the wild garlic and cook until it is just wilted and soft. Don't overcook it – wild garlic should be bright and vibrant. Taste and adjust the seasoning if necessary. This curry should be soft, fragrant, gently sweet, sharp and salty, with just enough heat to warm you…

Grilled rabbit with lentils cooked in red wine

I love rabbit, specifically farmed rabbit, which has a gentle, clean flavour – less gamey than wild rabbit – and doesn't come riddled with shot. Here I've grilled the legs, which respond well to quick cooking, and served them on a bed of earthy lentils – cooked in red wine with lots of flavourings. These full-bodied lentils are equally good with simply roasted chicken or grilled wild salmon, or tossed warm through a lightly dressed rocket and goat's cheese salad. *Illustrated on previous page*

Serves 4

4 farmed free-range rabbit legs (ask your butcher for meaty back legs)

sea salt and freshly ground black pepper

olive oil, to brush

Lentils in red wine

200g small Umbrian or Puy lentils

40ml olive oil

1 yellow onion, peeled and chopped

3 celery sticks, trimmed and chopped

3 carrots, peeled and chopped

4 slices of pancetta

small bunch of lemon thyme (or ordinary thyme)

3 bay leaves

2 garlic cloves, peeled and chopped

450ml full-bodied red wine, such as Barolo or Barbaresco

knob of butter

1 tbsp finely chopped parsley

Mustard and crème fraîche dressing

1/2 tbsp Dijon mustard

1 tsp sherry vinegar vinegar

200ml crème fraîche

First cook the lentils. Wash them well, drain and set aside. Heat the olive oil in a heavy-based pan, then add the onion, celery, carrots and pancetta. Cook gently over a low heat for 15 minutes or until the vegetables are soft and sweet. Add the lentils, thyme, bay leaves and garlic and stir well to combine.

Now pour in a third of the wine and turn up the heat slightly. Stir until the lentils have absorbed the wine, before adding another third (rather like making a risotto, but the wine is not added hot). When the second lot of wine is absorbed, add the rest. The lentils may still be a little hard once all the wine has been absorbed, in which case you'll need to add some water.

Continue cooking until the lentils are just tender to the bite – this may take as long as 40 minutes. Season well with salt and pepper and finish with the butter and chopped parsley. (You can prepare these lentils a few hours in advance.)

For the dressing, combine the mustard and sherry vinegar in a bowl, then whisk in the crème fraîche until smooth. Season with salt and pepper to taste.

When ready to serve, preheat the grill to high. Season the rabbit legs generously all over with salt and pepper and brush with olive oil. Lay them on the grill rack and grill on one side for 4 minutes, then turn and cook for 4 minutes on the other side. Check that the rabbit is cooked through.

To serve, spoon the lentils onto warm plates and lay a rabbit leg on each plate. Spoon over the mustard and crème fraîche dressing and serve at once.

Farinata

Farinata is a speciality of Genoa. A simple batter made of chick pea flour, it is traditionally baked in a wood-fired oven and served on its own, or with Gorgonzola dolce. I love it so much that I've even dreamt about eating it at night! Poor man's food – eaten by fishermen early in the morning before leaving on the day boats from Genoa harbour – it is hearty and sustaining.

Serves 6

225g chick pea flour

sea salt and freshly ground black pepper

4 tbsp extra virgin olive oil, preferably Ligurian, plus extra to serve

few rosemary sprigs, leaves only, chopped (optional)

225ml sparkling water

1 tbsp olive oil

Gorgonzola dolce, to serve (optional)

Put the chick pea flour into a bowl with 1 tsp salt and a little pepper and make a well. Pour in the extra virgin olive oil, and add the chopped rosemary if using, then whisk in the water. Mix until you have a smooth batter, then set aside to rest for 20 minutes.

Preheat the oven to 200°C/Gas 6. Place a large non-stick ovenproof frying pan over a medium heat. When hot, add 1 tbsp olive oil and swirl the pan to ensure that the base is evenly coated. Gently ladle in the batter, turn down the heat slightly and cook for 1–2 minutes.

Now transfer the pan to the middle shelf of the oven and bake, without turning, for 15 minutes or until the pancake is cooked through and golden brown.

Slide the hot farinata onto a plate and cut into rough triangles. If serving with Gorgonzola, top with the cheese and drizzle with a little extra virgin olive oil. Sprinkle a little salt and pepper over the farinata and serve warm.

Chick pea flour is available from most good delicatessens and specialist Middle Eastern food shops. Seek out a good-quality brand.

Tomatoes

There is something undeniably wonderful about the sharp, green smell of a tomato plant come midsummer. Put your nose up close to the vine and breathe in. The smell is quite unique – grassy, slightly peppery, pungent and completely summery. In a way, it is a strange smell but I love it. For me, tomatoes are one of the great joys of a summer menu – whether they are properly ripe, soft, sweet and fruity, or still green with a sharp flavour and tight, crunchy flesh. They come in all shapes and sizes – small and round, oval or teardrop, or the shape and size of an ox heart. And in a myriad of hues, from almost chocolate brown – through orange and yellow, striped and green – to perfectly ripe and gloriously red. Heritage tomatoes, San Marzano, cherry, datterini, tiger and cuore di bue are some of my favourite varieties.

When perfectly ripe and sweet, you can eat tomatoes in the manner of the fruit they are – just like an apple or pear – but perhaps with a pinch of sea salt. At their best, they need nothing else.

Although it is possible to buy tomatoes all year round, I encourage you to respect their season – midsummer to early autumn is when they are truly at their best. Silky, fragrant and plump at this time of year, their flavour more than makes up for the months they are not in season. Tomatoes that grace supermarket shelves all year round tend to be of the dependable growing varieties such as Moneymaker. Sadly they rarely have more than a hint of flavour; bland and watery, they add little to any dish.

Instead, look in season for tomatoes that feel heavy for their size and just yield to the touch. Avoid buying fruit that is too soft. The colour – whatever it may be – should be even and free of bruises and blemishes. Always keep tomatoes out of the fridge, as the cold arrests their perfume and flavour, and prevents them from reaching their full potential. Tomatoes that have over-ripened or begun to soften need not be wasted, however, as they can easily be made into a delicious tomato sauce for pasta (see right).

◊

Tomatoes have a natural affinity with nearly all herbs. The classic marriage of perfectly ripe tomatoes and basil is difficult to beat, but in early autumn try tomatoes with the earthy flavour of sage; marjoram, rosemary and oregano also work beautifully. Seasoning is very important. The crystal crunch of good-quality sea salt is the perfect foil for sweet tomato flesh – provided you use just the right amount. Olive oil – extra virgin – enhances the flavour, too. Really sweet tomatoes can take the more peppery olive oils. And a drizzle of good-quality red wine vinegar, or viscous, mellow traditional balsamic is the perfect foil for their sweetness.

Cheese, as I am sure you know, has a happy partnership with tomatoes. Sharp young goat's cheese, crumbly sheep's milk cheese and the freshest, softest, gentlest, buffalo mozzarella all work perfectly. Olives, capers and anchovies love tomatoes, too. Finally please don't forget their affinity with seafood – crab and lobster, in particular. Try the recipe on page 132... it is one of my favourites.

Slow-roasted tomatoes

These tomatoes have a delicious sweet, intense flavour. I add them to all kinds of dishes, including salads, vegetables, fish, red meat and cheeses. They will keep in the fridge for up to a month.

Makes 1 jar

6–8 ripe San Marzano or other plum tomatoes

10g caster sugar

10g sea salt

10g freshly ground black pepper

Preheat the oven to its lowest setting – probably 100°C/ Gas 1/4. Halve the tomatoes lengthways and lay them, cut side up, in a single layer on a large baking tray. Mix together the sugar, salt and pepper, then sprinkle over the cut surface of the tomatoes. Roast in the oven, undisturbed, for 3–4 hours until they shrivel up. Remove and leave to cool.

Refrigerate and use within a few days, or pack in sterilised jars, cover with extra virgin olive oil, seal and store in the fridge.

Tomato sauce for pasta

There is nothing fancy about this sauce. It's just incredibly useful – and a good way to use less than perfect tomatoes. It keeps well in the fridge for 3–4 days. Alternatively, you can store it in sterilised sealed jars in the fridge for a month or two, but use within a few days once opened.

Makes about 1 litre

1.5kg very ripe tomatoes

120ml extra virgin olive oil

1 large red onion, peeled and finely chopped

3 garlic cloves, peeled and crushed

sea salt and freshly ground black pepper

3 bay leaves

4–5 thyme sprigs

1 dried red chilli

Chop the tomatoes roughly, cutting away any blemishes and the stem. Warm the olive oil in a large, heavy-based pan over a low heat, add the onion and sweat gently for 10 minutes until soft, stirring occasionally. Add the garlic, a good pinch of salt, the bay leaves and thyme. Crumble in the dried chilli and cook for a further 5 minutes.

Add the tomatoes, stir well and turn the heat up. Cook fairly rapidly for 20 minutes, stirring frequently to ensure the sauce doesn't catch on the bottom of the pan and burn. To achieve a rich, vibrant sauce, you need to cook it over a high heat to evaporate the liquid; if it is too watery it will taste bland and thin. Taste and season with a little more salt if necessary and a few grindings of black pepper. Toss the sauce through cooked pasta to serve.

Sauce vierge

This is a classic French tomato vinaigrette, comprising diced ripe tomatoes, good olive oil, tarragon, basil and one of my very favourite herbs – chervil. The beauty of this sauce lies in its fresh clean flavour and it really needs to be put together shortly before serving. It goes beautifully with simply grilled fish of any variety, especially salmon and very fresh, deliciously oily sardines. It is also very good with grilled beef or lamb.

Makes about 750ml

1kg ripe, firm tomatoes, without bruises or blemishes

sea salt and freshly ground black pepper

bunch of chervil, leaves only

bunch of tarragon, leaves only

small bunch of basil, leaves only

1 tbsp good-quality red wine vinegar

120ml extra virgin olive oil

Put a large pot of water on to boil. Using a little knife, mark a shallow cross in the tomato skin – don't cut too deeply, it should really only be a nick. Plunge the tomatoes into the boiling water and remove them almost immediately (after about 15 seconds), using a slotted spoon. The skin at the cross incision should have curled back. Once they are cool enough to handle, peel off the skin – it should come away very easily. Halve the tomatoes, scoop out and discard the seeds, then cut into small, neat slices.

Put the tomato slices into a bowl and season well with salt and pepper. Chop the herbs finely and add them to the tomatoes. Drizzle over the wine vinegar, stir to combine, then pour over the olive oil. Use the sauce within an hour or two.

Tomato and bread soup

We make this soup in the early autumn when there tends to be a glut of tomatoes in the vegetable garden and we are anxious not to waste any. Inevitably some are in less than perfect condition – softening around the edges perhaps, or with the odd bruise or blemish. These are best showcased in this lovely, nurturing, elegantly flavoured soup. Based on the Tuscan *pappa al pomodoro*, it is a firm favourite of mine. This one is laced with garlic and sage, with just a hint of chilli, but you could replace the sage with basil for a more traditional flavour if you prefer.

Serves 4–6

1kg ripe tomatoes

80ml good-quality extra virgin olive oil, plus extra to drizzle

3 garlic cloves, peeled and sliced into fine slivers

1 dried red chilli

5 sage sprigs

sea salt and freshly ground black pepper

3 slices of day-old, chewy, peasant-style bread

aged balsamic vinegar, to finish (optional)

Chop the tomatoes roughly, but don't bother to remove the seeds. Place a heavy-based pan over a medium heat and add the olive oil. When the oil is warm but not hot, add the chopped tomatoes, garlic, chilli and sage. Season with a good pinch of sea salt and a couple of grindings of black pepper. Turn the heat to really low and cook for 40 minutes, stirring every now and then.

Tear the bread into rough chunks with your fingers and add to the soup. Don't stir though, just let the bread disintegrate into the soup – it will readily absorb the wonderful, deep, satisfying flavour of the cooked tomatoes.

Ladle into soup plates and drizzle with a little more olive oil and the balsamic vinegar if you wish. This soup is best served warm, rather than hot.

Nectarine and tomato salad with Parma ham and buffalo mozzarella

Nectarine with tomato may seem an odd combination for a salad, but it is actually quite exquisite. As with all simple things, it relies heavily on the use of very good ingredients. The nectarines should be sweet and properly ripe, the tomatoes the same. Texturally it is a lovely salad – soft and very refreshing on a hot summer's day. It should be served just on the cool side of room temperature.

Serves 4

4 perfectly ripe nectarines

20 perfectly ripe little tomatoes, such as San Marzano, datterini or cherry tomatoes

few drops of lemon juice

20ml (or so) of good-quality extra virgin olive oil

sea salt and freshly ground black pepper

4 balls of buffalo mozzarella

12 basil leaves (ideally purple basil), shredded

8 fine slices of Parma ham

2 tbsp basil oil (see below)

aged balsamic vinegar, to drizzle (optional)

Cut the nectarines in half along their natural division, remove the stones, then cut each half into thin wedges. Halve the tomatoes. Place the nectarines and tomatoes in a bowl and sprinkle with a few drops of lemon juice. Drizzle over the extra virgin olive oil and season with a little salt and pepper.

Tear the mozzarella balls in half with your fingers and lay 2 halves on each plate. Now build your salad, alternating the nectarine slices and tomatoes with basil and Parma ham, spooning a little basil oil between the layers and seasoning delicately as you go. Finish with a restrained drizzle of balsamic vinegar if you like.

Serve at once, preferably with some really good chewy peasant-style bread drizzled with olive oil.

Basil oil is a vibrant, sludgy sauce

that I use to finish many dishes. To make it, whiz the leaves from 3 large bunches of basil in a food processor with 1 peeled garlic clove and a good pinch each of salt and pepper until the basil is finely chopped. With the motor running, slowly trickle in 200ml extra virgin olive oil through the funnel and blend until you have a beautiful green purée. Let stand for a few minutes, then taste and adjust the seasoning. Store in a jar in the fridge – it will keep for up to a week.

Squash and tomato curry with lime and coconut

This curry is full of big, bold, clean, clear flavours. I love the strength of its colour – it looks warm and inviting, happy and confident on the plate. It is good eaten with any type of flat bread and a tangle of blanched chard or spinach leaves dressed with a squeeze of lime juice and a drop or two of olive oil. Onion squash comes into season early September and is around right through the autumn. It is not the sweetest of the squash varieties, but it has a richness and depth of flavour that is quite unique. Don't bother to peel off the skin – it is best left on.

Serves 4

1 medium onion squash

1 tbsp vegetable oil

1 red onion, peeled and finely sliced

3 garlic cloves, peeled and finely chopped

1 green chilli, chopped (seeds left in)

10 curry leaves

bunch of coriander, roots and stalks finely sliced, leaves reserved for garnish

1 tsp mustard seeds

1 tsp fennel seeds

2 tbsp caster sugar, or to taste

2 tbsp fish sauce, or to taste

juice of 2 limes, or to taste

15–20 ripe little tomatoes, such as San Marzano

340g jar (or tinned) good-quality peeled plum tomatoes

250ml coconut milk (fresh or tinned)

Using a large, very sharp knife, slice through the middle of the onion squash. Scoop out the seeds using a spoon, then slice into 5cm wedges and set aside.

Place a heavy-based pan over a medium heat. Add the oil and when it is warm, add the onion. Lower the heat and cook for 10 minutes until soft and translucent. Add the garlic, chilli, curry leaves and the coriander roots and stalks, and continue to cook gently.

Meanwhile, warm a small, non-stick frying pan over a medium heat, add the mustard and fennel seeds and cook until they just begin to pop – the heat will tickle out their. Remove from the heat and pound to a powder, using a pestle and mortar. Add to the onion curry base, stir to combine and cook gently for a further 5 minutes.

Add the onion squash, stir again and cook for 10 minutes, then add the sugar, fish sauce and lime juice. It is really important to get the balance of flavours right at this stage, so now is the time to taste and assess. The curry should be pleasantly (not aggressively) hot; sweet (but not sickly); sour (but not so much that it makes you squint); and salty enough to underpin and ground the dish.

Once you feel the flavours are just right, add the little ripe tomatoes – squishing them slightly between your fingers as you do so, to help them release their lovely flavour. Add the jar of plum tomatoes, too. Cook for a further 20–25 minutes until the squash is tender when pierced with a fork. Pour in the coconut milk and cook for a final 5 minutes or so.

The tomato and coconut milk enrich the curry, giving it a depth and smoothness that complete the dish. Turn off the heat and allow to cool. Reheat the curry gently and thoroughly when you are ready to serve. Like many wet dishes, this one improves in flavour if allowed to cool and sit before reheating.

Lobster with white beans, tarragon and tomatoes

I find the sweet, rich flesh of lobsters a real treat to eat. We cook this dish primarily during the early months of summer, when small native lobsters are particularly good. Perfectly ripe cooked tomatoes and tarragon, with its faintly aniseed flavour, make it really special.

Serves 4

4 small live lobsters, about 500g each

300g podded fresh white cannellini beans, or pre-soaked good-quality dried ones

40ml extra virgin olive oil

1 garlic clove, peeled and crushed

bunch of tarragon, leaves only

1 tbsp red wine vinegar

20 perfectly ripe little tomatoes, such as San Marzano, datterini or cherry tomatoes

sea salt and freshly ground black pepper

100ml Pernod

knob of butter

Put the lobsters into the freezer for an hour or two, to render them soporific. Then, to par-cook them, place the lobsters in a pan and pour in enough cold water to cover them by about 15cm. Turn the heat up as high as it will go and cook until the water is on the point of boiling. Turn off the heat and let the lobsters sit in the hot water for 1 minute. Using tongs, remove them and allow to cool.

Have a bowl to hand so you can tip in and save the delicious juices as you prepare the lobsters. Lay one on its back and slice down the middle from top to tail with a sharp knife. Remove the meat from the body and set aside on a plate. Twist off the small legs, cutting off and discarding the bits of feathery gill sticking to the knuckle ends. Lay the legs alongside the body. Twist off the claws, then using a pair of scissors, cut down the length of the arms and pull out the meat. Crack the claws with a mallet and gently remove the shell – to remove the flesh in one piece. Set aside with the rest of the meat. Repeat with the other lobsters. Now you can start cooking…

Preheat the oven to 180°C/Gas 4. Tip the beans into a baking dish, pour in the olive oil and add water to cover generously. Stir in the garlic, half the tarragon and the wine vinegar. Now add the tomatoes, piercing each one with a sharp knife as you do so, to let their sweet juice ooze out during cooking. Season with salt, cover and place in the oven. Cook until the beans are creamy and tender; about 35–40 minutes for fresh beans, around $1^1/4$ hours for dried ones. Check the liquid from time to time, adding a little more water if needed. Once tender, set aside while you warm the lobster.

Pour the Pernod into a saucepan large enough to hold the lobster meat and warm over a low heat. Add the lobster and reserved juices and warm through briefly, turning occasionally to ensure it is evenly heated. Remove with a slotted spoon and divide among warm bowls.

Turn up the heat under the pan to high and add the butter, whisking vigorously to combine. Add to the warm beans, stir in the remaining tarragon and taste for seasoning. Ladle over the lobster and serve immediately. Grilled sourdough bread – rubbed with a whisper of garlic and brushed with the best quality olive oil – is perfect for mopping up the juices.

Sea bass with mint, tomatoes and red onions

This is lovely, simple way to serve filleted small fish. Use the sweetest possible onions and the ripest tomatoes. The addition of mint is surprising and delicious, giving the dish a fresh, clean taste. Get your fishmonger to clean, scale and gut the fish for you, and to fillet it as well if you can.

Serves 4

4 sea bass fillets with skin, about 180g each

100ml extra virgin olive oil

3 sweet red onions, peeled and finely sliced

1 tsp fennel seeds

1 dried red chilli

sea salt and freshly ground black pepper

handful of flat leaf parsley, leaves only, coarsely chopped

small bunch of mint, leaves only, coarsely chopped

4 ripe, sweet, juicy tomatoes, roughly chopped

1 tbsp sherry vinegar

1 tbsp olive oil, for frying

Season the skin of fish generously

and cook until it is crunchy. I urge you to eat the skin of all fish. When perfectly cooked it adds an element to the final taste that completes the dish.

Set the sea bass fillets aside on a covered plate to allow them to come to room temperature.

Place a pan over a low heat, pour in the extra virgin olive oil and, when the oil is warm, add the onions. Cook very gently for about 30 minutes, to bring out the gentle sweetness of the onions. Meanwhile, toast the fennel seeds in a dry frying pan to release their flavour, then grind using a pestle and mortar.

Add the ground fennel seeds to the onions, crumble in the chilli and season with a little salt. Cook for a further 10 minutes, still over a very low heat. Add half the parsley and mint, stir well, then add the tomatoes and sherry vinegar. Turn up the heat a little and cook for 10 minutes. This sauce should taste very clean, so don't cook the tomatoes for too long.

Preheat the oven to 180°C/Gas 4. Season the fish well, especially on the skin side. Place a non-stick ovenproof frying pan over a high heat. Pour in a little olive oil and when hot, lay the fish skin side down in the pan. Cook for 2–3 minutes until the skin is golden brown. Immediately transfer the pan to the oven to finish cooking without turning the fish. This should take no more than a further 2–3 minutes.

To serve, taste the sauce for seasoning and adjust if necessary, then add the rest of the parsley and mint. Spoon into warm shallow bowls and lay the fish fillets on top. Serve at once.

Rabbit with saffron, cucumber, tomatoes and basil

I'm very partial to rabbit and it is always a popular choice when we have it on the menu, yet sadly it seems to be underrated in this country. This combination, inspired by a dish in Richard Olney's *Simple French Food*, is exquisite. For hefty appetites, you might like to cook the smaller shoulders along with the legs – they have a lovely sweet flavour. We serve this dish with soft polenta laced with lemon zest, unsalted butter, black pepper and Parmesan.

Serves 6

6 farmed free-range rabbit legs (and shoulders, if you like)

sea salt and freshly ground black pepper

2 tbsp olive oil

40 saffron threads

3 garlic cloves, peeled and finely sliced

750ml verjuice

20 little ripe tomatoes, such as San Marzano, datterini, or cherry tomatoes

4 little cucumbers

bunch of basil, leaves only

large knob of unsalted butter

Season the rabbit portions with salt and pepper. Place a large, wide pan over a medium heat and add the olive oil. When it is hot, brown the rabbit in batches if necessary; don't overcrowd the pan. You want to brown the portions quite gently, but really thoroughly until they are golden brown all over.

Add the saffron and garlic, then pour in the verjuice, scraping up all the delicious juices from the bottom of the pan. Allow to bubble to reduce down a bit, then turn the heat to low. Using the tip of a sharp knife, pierce each tomato and add to the pan. Season with a little more salt and pepper, then cover and cook gently for 30 minutes until the rabbit is cooked through. Continue to cook slowly for a further 15 minutes until the rabbit is very tender.

Meanwhile, half the cucumbers lengthways and scoop out the seeds, then halve each piece or cut into quarters. Add to the rabbit and cook for no more than a couple of minutes. Tear the basil into strips with your fingers and add to the pan along with the knob of butter. Swirl to combine and immediately remove from the heat. Taste one last time and adjust the seasoning if you need to, then serve.

Rabbit takes well to quick cooking – on a grill, for example. Equally it responds well to long slow cooking over a gentle heat. It is the indecisive in between cooking that can sometimes make it tough.

Lamb with tomatoes, chard and horseradish dressing

This recipe showcases *cuore di bue*, large tomatoes from Italy the size and shape of an ox heart, hence the name. I prefer to use these tomatoes still slightly green, when their flavour is pleasantly sharp and refreshing. Here I combine them with grilled lamb and my favourite chard. I love all greens but, to me, nothing is nicer than properly cooked tender rainbow or Swiss chard with a good glug of olive oil – it tastes as if it is so good for you!

Serves 6

1 boned leg of English lamb, trimmed of most of its fat and cut into 6 generous slices

sea salt and freshly ground black pepper

500g rainbow chard, washed

50ml extra virgin olive oil

2–3cm piece fresh horseradish, peeled

4 tbsp red wine vinegar

olive oil, to brush

2 *cuore di bue* tomatoes, cut into 3mm thick slices

Heat up your barbecue or grill, as it needs to be really hot in order to give the lamb a lovely strong crust and flavour.

Bring a large pot of well-salted water to the boil. Plunge the chard into the boiling water and cook for 2–3 minutes, then drain in a colander (but don't refresh). Dress while warm with the extra virgin olive oil and season with a little salt and pepper. Set aside until you are ready to serve.

Grate the horseradish, place in a small bowl and pour over the wine vinegar. Season with a little salt (but no pepper) and set aside.

Brush the lamb with olive oil and season generously with salt and pepper. Lay on the barbecue or under the hot grill and cook for 3 minutes without moving, then turn the slices and cook on the other side for 3 minutes. Remove to a plate and set aside in a warm place to rest for 5 minutes or so.

To serve, cut the lamb into 1cm thick slices. Lay a slice of tomato on each plate, arrange a little chard on top, then add a slice of lamb and spoon over a little horseradish dressing. Continue layering until the lamb, chard and tomatoes are all used. This dish is best served at room temperature.

Food eaten at room temperature is one of the best ways to experience subtle nuances of flavour. For me, it is the ideal way to experience many tastes – perhaps that's why I am so fond of salads.

Tomato and apple ketchup

At the beginning of autumn, when the last of the summer tomatoes
are still around and the earliest apples are creeping in, it is time
to make ketchup. Good homemade tomato ketchup is a delight.
Sweet and zingy, it is the perfect accompaniment to grilled beef
or hamburgers, sharp English Cheddars and lemony goat's cheeses
– though you only need a tiny amount with these delicately
flavoured soft cheeses.

Makes 1 large jar

1 tbsp olive oil

5 red onions, peeled and
roughly chopped

1kg apples

2.5kg ripe tomatoes

2 garlic cloves, peeled and
finely chopped

400g caster sugar

500ml red wine vinegar

10 cloves

2 cinnamon sticks

3 bay leaves

12 juniper berries

sea salt and freshly ground
black pepper

Place a preserving pan or a large heavy-based saucepan on a low heat
and add the olive oil. When it is warm, tip in the onions and sweat
gently for 10 minutes until soft and translucent. Meanwhile, core
and roughly chop (but do not peel) the apples and tomatoes.

Add the garlic to the pan and sweat for a minute, the add the apples
and tomatoes. Stir in the sugar and red wine vinegar. Tie the spices,
bay leaves and juniper berries in a piece of muslin and drop into the
pan. Stir the mixture to combine all the ingredients, then turn the
heat to low and cook gently for 1$\frac{1}{2}$ hours, stirring occasionally to
make sure the mixture doesn't stick on the bottom of the pan.

The ketchup is ready when it has cooked right down to a glossy,
pulpy sauce. Add a generous pinch of salt and a few grindings of
pepper, to taste. Allow to cool, then spoon into one large or two
small sterilised jars. Seal and store in a cool, dark place. Use within
a few months and keep in the fridge once opened.

Made in generous quantities and stored in sterilised jars,
this ketchup will keep happily in the fridge or cool, dark larder
throughout the autumn and even into the start of winter – providing a
taste of warmth to dishes in the cooler months.

Nuts

Last autumn, on a warm, sunny day, I had the most unforgettable simple lunch on a lavender farm just outside Melbourne. The crop was being harvested and the heady scent of lavender was everywhere. A table was laid under a huge, old walnut tree and all around underfoot were young pale coloured walnuts. Their shells broke effortlessly. Crisp to the bite and very sweet, these beautiful nuts were a memorable taste and a joyful reminder of the turning of the season.

Nuts provide both textural depth and flavour to dishes in a way that nothing else is really quite able to. I love this quality and use all sorts of nuts in my cooking, especially during autumn and winter. Young, sweet hazelnuts and cobnuts are among my favourites... and creamy fresh walnuts of course. As with all nuts, freshness is of the utmost importance, so buy them in the shell if you possibly can – and treat them with respect, as they are delicate and easily spoilt.

Sadly, nuts are often not at their peak when they arrive in the shops for us to buy. Although regarded as a storecupboard ingredient, they are fragile and perishable, soon losing their freshness and turning rancid. So, wherever possible, nuts should be bought in their shell, in small quantities, and kept in a sealed container in a cool dark place. They really need to be eaten within a couple of weeks of purchase, at the most.

Walnuts are probably the most delicate of all nuts. Their flavour declines rapidly once they are removed from their shell, turning bitter and sharp. Sweet, creamy 'wet walnuts' as they are known when young and fresh, are altogether different and probably the best crop of the year.

◊

Different nut varieties work better with different ingredients. You may well have your own ideas and preferences, but here is my rough guide to pairing nuts with other foods:

Almonds work well with chocolate, honey, peaches, nectarines and apricots. They are also lovely with delicate pink-fleshed fish like trout and salmon, but also with rabbit and succulent little birds such as pigeon or quail. In Spain, ground or finely chopped almonds are often used to thicken dishes, providing texture as well as a creamy, sweet richness.

Hazelnuts are beautiful with many cheeses, especially hard cow's milk cheeses, but also in a salad with warm game and pickled fruit. Pounded into a thick paste and laced with orange zest, they will enhance grilled pork, beef and lamb. And, of course, hazelnuts are perfect with chocolate and honey.

Chestnuts are lovely with meringues, icing sugar and cream. In savoury dishes, they work well with Parma ham, sage, game birds, porcini, potatoes, Brussels sprouts and winter greens.

Pine nuts go with basil, Parmesan, pecorino and olive oil to make pesto, obviously, but also with pasta, spinach, raisins, quail and most salad leaves.

Cashews, candlenuts and peanuts have a natural affinity with chilli, tamarind, mint, coriander, cucumber, lime, coconut milk, white fish, chicken and white rice.

Pecans go well with maple syrup, cream, bananas and caramel, as well as blue cheeses, dates, beetroot and avocados.

Walnuts are lovely with crisp sweet apples and pears, blue cheeses, game, watercress and other bitter greens. And when creamy and fresh, they are sublime pounded into a paste with garlic, lemon zest and parsley, or breadcrumbs, roasted tomatoes and dried chillies to serve with meat or white fish.

◊

Whenever you are serving nuts or using them in cooking, first warm or toast them gently in the oven to tickle out their flavour, if not too colour them. The heat of the oven heightens their taste and fragrance and gives them a better bite. Lastly, when grinding nuts, do use a pestle and mortar to pound them. To my mind, a blender or food processor is too aggressive for nuts and spoils their flavour.

Nut oils feature strongly in my cooking during the autumn. I love to drizzle walnut or hazelnut oil over grilled lamb or beef, and these oils are charming with leaves such as frisée, mâche and watercress.

Salad of roasted beetroot, walnuts, watercress and mascarpone

I love the gentle sweetness of beetroot – they taste to me quite simply of the earth from which they have been pulled. My favourite way to cook them is roasted in their skins, while they are still young and small. Warm from the oven, they work so nicely with walnuts and watercress. This salad makes a good first course or you can serve it as part of a larger spread.

Serves 4

12 small beetroot

1 tbsp aged balsamic vinegar

2 tbsp olive oil

sea salt and freshly ground black pepper

generous handful of watercress, trimmed

20 creamy young 'wet' walnuts in the shell

160–180g mascarpone

squeeze of lemon juice

2 tsp aged balsamic vinegar

4 tbsp walnut oil

Preheat the oven to 180°C/Gas 4. Wash the beetroot well to remove any dirt, but leave their skins on. If they have little roots, leave them on as they create a lovely heap on the plate.

Place the beetroot in a roasting tray and drizzle over the balsamic vinegar and olive oil. Season with salt and pepper and cover the tray tightly with the foil. Roast on the middle shelf of the oven for 35 minutes, then remove the foil and cook for a further 15 minutes or until the skins are wrinkly and the beetroot feel tender when pierced with a skewer.

Meanwhile, wash the watercress and pat dry. Crack the walnuts and remove them from their shells. Arrange the watercress and warm beetroot on individual plates. Spoon the mascarpone on top and squeeze over the lemon juice, with a light touch.

Scatter the walnuts over the salad, then drizzle over the aged balsamic and walnut oil. Season with salt and pepper and serve, while the beetroot are still just warm.

The importance of texture in cooking cannot be underestimated. All things must be considered on tasting – flavour first and always, but also how the food feels in your mouth.

Roasted Jerusalem artichokes with goat's cheese, roasted tomatoes and agresto

Agresto is a soft, rounded, pounded paste made with very fresh, young, creamy walnuts. It works exceptionally well with the rich, nutty flavour of roasted Jerusalem artichokes and sweet lightly roasted tomatoes. The goat's cheese lends a gentle lemony acidity, which rounds the dish off a treat.

Serves 4

12 Jerusalem artichokes

4 tbsp olive oil

sea salt and freshly ground black pepper

12 little plum or cherry tomatoes

1/2 tbsp good-quality red wine vinegar

4 slices of chewy peasant-style bread

1 garlic clove, peeled

drizzle of extra virgin olive oil

pinch of sea salt

generous handful of salad leaves, such as cicorino or rocket

200g young, light goat's cheese, such as fleur de chèvre

Agresto

20 young 'wet' walnuts in the shell

2 good-quality salted anchovy fillets

1 garlic clove, peeled

1 dried red chilli, finely chopped

1 small bunch of flat leaf parsley, leaves only, chopped

finely grated zest and juice of 1 lemon

200ml extra virgin olive oil

First make the agresto. Crack open the walnuts (I give them a gentle tap with a rolling pin) and extract the nuts. Place a handful of them in a large mortar and start to pound gently with the pestle, gradually adding the rest of the nuts. Add the anchovies and garlic and continue to pound – the sauce should be smooth and creamy in parts, roughly textured in others. Stir in the chilli, parsley, lemon zest and juice, then gradually incorporate the extra virgin olive oil. Taste and adjust the seasoning – adding a little salt if necessary and a good grinding of pepper. Set aside while you roast the artichokes.

Preheat the oven to 200°C/Gas 6. Scrub the artichokes under cold running water to remove the dirt, but don't bother to peel them. Cut in half lengthways and place in a roasting tray. Drizzle over 3 tbsp of the olive oil, season generously with salt and pepper and toss to coat well. Roast on the middle shelf of the oven until the artichokes are golden brown and tender; this will take about 35–40 minutes.

Halfway through cooking the artichokes, place the tomatoes in a separate roasting pan, season and spoon over the wine vinegar and 1 tbsp olive oil. Roast on the top shelf of the oven for about 15 minutes until the tomatoes are soft and beginning to split from their skins. Set aside in a warm place with the artichokes while you toast the bread.

Preheat the grill and toast the slices of bread until golden brown on both sides. Once the bread is a really good colour, remove from the grill and rub gently on one side with the garlic. Drizzle with a little extra virgin olive oil and season with salt.

Place a slice of bruschetta on each plate. Arrange the artichokes, salad leaves and tomatoes on top and crumble over the goat's cheese. Spoon on the agresto and serve at once, while still warm.

Squid with rocket and romesco

Romesco is one of the great nut-based sauces of Spain. We serve it in all sorts of ways – with simple grilled meats or game; seafood such as sautéed prawns with wilted spinach; even scattered over grilled spicy chorizo with a handful of lightly dressed rocket. Romesco can be based on almonds alone but adding hazelnuts gives the sauce a more complex flavour. It is best used on the day it is made.

Serves 4

500g small squid, with tentacles

sea salt and freshly ground black pepper

40ml olive oil

Salad

small handful of mint, leaves only

small handful of basil, leaves only

generous handful of rocket leaves

juice of 1 lemon

50–60ml extra virgin olive oil

Romesco

50g shelled almonds

30g shelled hazelnuts

2 ripe tomatoes

1 large red chilli

4 garlic cloves, peeled

1 tsp sweet paprika

1 tbsp good-quality red wine vinegar

4 tbsp fresh course white breadcrumbs

100ml extra virgin olive oil

To serve

lemon wedges

To clean the squid, hold the body with one hand and pull out the head with the tentacles attached, using the other hand; most of the innards will come too. Peel off the skin at the same time. Cut the tentacles from the head, discarding the head, eyes and hard beak. Remove the transparent quill from the body and the soft gooey matter. Rinse the body pouch and tentacles gently under cold running water, drain and set aside in a cool place.

For the romesco, preheat the oven to 180°C/Gas 4. Place the nuts on a baking tray and roast on the middle oven shelf for 5–6 minutes until evenly golden. Tip the hot nuts into a clean dry cloth and rub to remove the skins. Place the tomatoes and chilli on a baking tray and roast for about 10 minutes, turning halfway through cooking, until the tomatoes are slightly coloured and bursting from their skins, and the chilli is soft – it might take an extra minute or two.

Put the garlic and a pinch of salt into a large mortar and crush with the pestle to a rough paste, then add the chilli and crush. Add the roasted nuts and pound until the paste is fairly smooth, but still retains some texture. Add the tomatoes and paprika and continue to pound, but more gently now. Stir in the wine vinegar, breadcrumbs and finally the extra virgin olive oil. Season to taste and set aside.

For the salad, wash the herb and salad leaves, pat dry and place in a large bowl. Drizzle over the lemon juice and extra virgin olive oil, season with salt and pepper and toss lightly to combine.

Heat one large or two smaller non-stick frying pans over a fairly high heat. Season the squid well all over and add a little olive oil to the pan(s). Once the oil is hot, add the squid being careful not to overcrowd the pan. Cook undisturbed for 1 minute, then turn and cook for a minute on the other side.

Tip the squid into the bowl of dressed leaves and toss to combine the flavours. Arrange on warm plates and crumble over the romesco. Serve immediately, with lemon wedges for squeezing.

Skirt steak
is a less
common cut
of beef, but it has
an excellent flavour
and is well worth
seeking out. A lean
cut from the inner
thigh with elongated
fibres, it's best served
rare, sliced against
the grain.

Skirt steak with hazelnut picada and wilted escarole

Picada hails from Spain, or more specifically, from Catalonia. Flavoured with nuts, breadcrumbs and herbs, it is a punchy, vibrant paste – often used as a sauce to enliven dishes, and to thicken stews. Here it partners full-favoured skirt steak and elegant escarole lettuce, which is just wilted to serve as a vegetable. Like romesco, there are plenty of other uses for picada, if you have any leftover.

Serves 4

700g skirt steak, cut into
4 portions

1 head of escarole

sea salt and freshly ground
black pepper

a little extra virgin olive oil

50g unsalted butter

Picada

1 thick slice of chewy peasant-
style bread

180ml extra virgin olive oil

20 shelled hazelnuts

grated or finely shredded zest
of 1 orange

1 tbsp orange juice

1 garlic clove, peeled

small bunch of oregano,
leaves only

Set the steaks aside on a covered plate to bring them to room temperature.

For the picada, preheat the oven to 180°C/Gas 4. Tear the bread roughly into pieces. Heat the olive oil in a shallow pan over a medium heat. When it is hot, add the bread and fry until evenly golden and crisp. (Take care that the olive oil does not become too hot and begin to smoke.) Remove and drain off excess oil. Pound the bread, in batches if necessary, using a pestle and mortar, until you have coarse breadcrumbs.

Place the nuts on a baking tray and roast in the middle of the oven for 10 minutes until evenly golden. Tip the hot nuts into a clean dry cloth and rub to remove the skins. Finely chop the nuts and place in a bowl with the breadcrumbs, orange zest and juice. Finely chop the garlic and oregano together and add to the bowl with a pinch of salt. Stir to combine, then set aside. Turn the oven to its lowest setting.

Discard the outer leaves from the escarole, then tear the lettuce into large pieces. Wash well, but don't bother to pat dry.

Season the steaks liberally all over. Place a heavy-based frying pan over a high heat and brush the steaks with a little olive oil. Lay the steaks in the pan when it is hot and cook without moving for 3 minutes. Turn and cook on the other side for 3 minutes (you may need a minute or two longer if the steaks have been cut from a thicker section of the thigh). You should have a nice brown crust, while the meat inside should be rare. Remove to a plate and rest in the warm oven for 6–8 minutes.

Meanwhile, cook the escarole. Place a wide pan over a medium-low heat. Add the butter and let it just melt, then add the torn leaves and seasoning. Put the lid on until the water clinging to the leaves begins to steam, then uncover and stir every few seconds so the leaves wilt uniformly. This will take 2–3 minutes. Now you should have a lovely glossy, pale green vegetable. Check the seasoning.

Place a steak on each warm serving plate and arrange the escarole alongside. Spoon over the picada and serve at once.

Warm date and almond puddings

These cosy, warm little puddings are just the sort of thing I like to eat when the weather turns cool. Like most people, I tend to have dessert as an occasional treat, rather than as a regular occurrence; these, however, I find almost impossible to resist. I like to eat them warm and steaming with thick cold Jersey cream – and sometimes a spoonful of warm golden syrup, laced with freshly grated lemon and orange zest.

Serves 6

120g unsalted butter, plus extra to grease

plain flour, to dust

6 tbsp golden syrup, slightly warmed

12 Medjool dates

1 tbsp Pedro Ximénez sherry

120g caster sugar

2 organic free-range large eggs

60g self-raising flour

small pinch of salt

1 tsp baking powder

30g ground almonds

finely grated zest of 1 orange

Butter and flour 6 individual pudding bowls, of about 170ml capacity. Set on a baking tray and spoon 1 tbsp golden syrup into each of the moulds (this will become the sticky topping). Set aside.

Remove the stones from the dates and chop them into small pieces. Place in a bowl and add the sherry and just enough boiling water to cover. Leave to soak for 10 minutes.

Preheat the oven to 190°C/Gas 5. Cream the butter and sugar together either by hand or using an electric mixer until soft, light and creamy. Add the eggs, one by one, beating well after each addition. (The mixture may appear to separate at this point, but it will come back together.)

Sift together the flour, salt and baking powder, combine with the ground almonds and fold into the pudding mixture with the orange zest. Finally squeeze out the excess moisture from the dates, add to the mixture and stir well to combine.

Divide the mixture among the pudding bowls, filling them no more than two-thirds full. Bake in the oven for 25 minutes or until well risen, golden and springy to the touch.

To unmould, run a small knife around the inside of each mould and invert the pudding onto a warm plate. Serve the little puddings at once, either on their own or, as I prefer, with a dollop of cream.

Hazelnut tart

This is a simple tart – both in flavour and execution. These days I always make pastry in the food processor – it is so much quicker and less messy than mixing it by hand. I prepare this tart most often in the autumn, when the first nuts of the year begin to appear. My favourite way to serve it is with crème fraîche and sweet tender autumn raspberries.

Serves 8–10

Pastry

250g plain flour, sifted, plus extra to dust

125g unsalted butter

30g caster sugar

1 organic free-range egg

1 organic free-range egg yolk

finely grated zest of 1 unwaxed lemon

1/2 tsp vanilla extract

Filling

300g shelled hazelnuts

300g caster sugar

3 whole eggs

finely grated zest of 1 unwaxed lemon

300g unsalted butter, in pieces

For the pastry, have all the ingredients well chilled. Tip the flour into a food processor. Cut the butter into tiny cubes, or grate it if you prefer. Add to the flour along with the sugar, whole egg, egg yolk, lemon zest and vanilla extract. Now turn on the machine. The mixture will soon have a granular, moist texture, the consistency of wet sand. Keep going and it should soon gather into a ball. Just occasionally you may find you need to add a little iced water to help it along – do this sparingly as it is easy to over-do it. Take out the dough, wrap it in cling film and leave to rest in the fridge for 30 minutes or so while you make the filling.

Preheat the oven to 190°C/Gas 5. Place the nuts on a baking tray and roast on the middle shelf of the oven for 5–6 minutes – to tickle out their flavour and make the skins easier to remove. Tip the nuts into a clean dry cloth and rub the cloth between your hands – the skins should slip off, so you can discard them quite easily.

Place the nuts in a blender and add the sugar, eggs, lemon zest and butter. Pulse to combine – keeping the nuts quite textural, rather than grinding them finely. Transfer to a bowl and set aside.

Lightly flour your work surface and rolling pin and roll out the pastry to a large round, about 3mm thick. Lift the pastry onto the rolling pin and drape it over a 25cm flan tin, about 2.5cm deep, with removable base. Press the pastry into the edges and sides of the tin and prick the base all over with a fork. Place in the fridge for 30 minutes to rest.

Line the pastry case with greaseproof paper and baking beans and bake 'blind' for 15 minutes. Remove the beans and paper and return the pastry case to the oven for a further 5 minutes. Allow to cool slightly. Spoon in the hazelnut filling, distributing it evenly. Bake for 30–35 minutes until golden; the filling should still be just soft in the centre. If it appears to be overbrowning, cover loosely with foil.

Allow the tart to cool to room temperature before slicing and serving, either on its own or with crème fraîche and raspberries.

Pecan and maple syrup ice cream

I make ice cream every day of the year, even through the winter months. Clean, gentle and not too sweet, I find it is one of the nicest ways to finish a meal – light or heavy. No matter how bespoke some shop-bought ice creams claim to be, I find homemade ice cream far superior. This is one of the sweeter ice creams we make, which is probably why it is always popular with children. Pecans and maple syrup have a natural affinity.

Serves 8

500ml whole milk

1 vanilla pod, split lengthways

10 organic free-range egg yolks

100g caster sugar

1 1/2 tbsp maple syrup, plus extra to drizzle

300ml double cream

20 shelled pecan nuts, plus a few extra to serve, roughly chopped

Pour the milk into a heavy-based saucepan. Scrape the seeds from the vanilla pod and add them to the milk, together with the empty pod. Place over a low heat and slowly bring to just below the boil. Take off the heat and leave to infuse for at least 30 minutes. Remove the vanilla pod.

Put the eggs and sugar in a bowl and whisk together thoroughly. Return the milk to a medium-low heat. As soon as it comes to just under a boil, take off the heat and add the maple syrup. Pour onto the egg yolk mixture, stirring with the whisk as you do so.

Pour the mixture back into the saucepan and stir over a very low heat with a wooden spoon, using a figure-of-eight motion, until the custard has thickened enough to lightly coat the back of the spoon. Don't overheat or it may curdle. As soon as it thickens, remove from the heat, pour into a bowl and allow to cool completely.

Once cool, stir through the cream and churn in an ice-cream maker. When the ice cream begins to set, add the chopped pecan nuts and continue to churn for another 10 minutes. Transfer the ice cream to a freezerproof container and place in the freezer for at least 2 hours before serving. It is best served within a day or two of making.

To serve, scoop the ice cream into bowls, sprinkle with a few chopped pecans and add a drizzle of maple syrup.

An ice-cream maker is essential for smooth-textured ices and sorbets. You can now purchase relatively inexpensive machines for use in a domestic kitchen.

Vinegar

The sharp, clear, top note flavour of vinegar serves to hone and refine flavours in cooking. I use it as an enhancer in conjunction with other flavourings, to give a dish a sense of wholeness. In my cooking, vinegar is often married with the saltiness of anchovies, the warmth rather than heat of dried chillies, the lovely grassiness of olive oil, the fragrance of spices – such as fennel or coriander seeds – and base note herbs like sage and rosemary.

Vinegar, like olive oil or wine, has a host of different possibilities within its umbrella term – from thin and eye-squintingly sharp – to rich, viscous and mellow, and even sweet. More often than not I cook with the sharper vinegars – long, slow, gentle cooking softens the flavour, smoothing its edges. Of course, aged balsamic vinegar with its wonderfully complex, sweet flavour is in a class of its own. Just a few drops sprinkled onto a dish will impart a very special quality.

In my larder I have several different varieties of vinegar, including cider, honey, white wine and spiced vinegars, but the two I use most frequently are very good-quality red wine vinegar and sherry vinegar. I find sherry vinegar pairs beautifully with the first of the season's nut oils, especially hazelnut and walnut. In the autumn, sherry vinegar comes into its own in my kitchen, as I use it to make vinaigrettes to dress seasonal salads – comprising mushrooms, nuts, perhaps finely shaved fennel, some torn warm pheasant or pigeon, and maybe a few pickled autumn grapes.

Red wine vinegar, on the other hand, I use more often in cooking. A splash invariably goes into slow-cooked pork and lamb dishes. And I like to add a drop or two when roasting tomatoes or borlotti beans, or to flavour still-warm farro. On its own, the flavour can be too sharp, but paired with olive oil, herbs and other flavourings – even Parmesan and butter – really beautiful and profound flavours can be achieved.

Malt vinegar is one variety I don't use in my cooking – its flavour is achingly sharp and thin, and it lacks the depth of traditionally made wine vinegars. I appreciated the harsh taste more as a child – sprinkled onto potato scallops (deep-fried, battered potato slices) from our local fish shop, which I loved at the time. So the flavour lingers in my memory, happily and evocatively!

◊

Balsamic vinegar is produced in a different way from the wine- or sherry- based vinegars described above. The base for balsamic vinegar is what the Italians call *cotto mosto*, which is essentially crushed grapes that are cooked in copper pots. No flavourings or additives are added. Aged naturally, the vinegar ferments in a series of wooden casks that range from cherry and juniper to oak and chestnut – in no particular order. Each wooden cask contributes its very own flavour to the final complex, dark amber vinegar. The taste is not sharp at all. It is best described as mellow, round and sweet, with notes of honey, but still tasting very much of the grape from which it originated.

When buying balsamic vinegar, on the label look for the description *aceto balsamico tradizionale* – only this wording confirms the vinegar's authenticity. There are many poor imitations on the market that do not resemble the true product at all – sometimes no more than cheap vinegar flavoured with caramel. True aged balsamic vinegar is unquestionably costly, but well worth the expense. You only need to use it sparingly – a drop or two is often enough to give a dish special character.

Good-quality vinegars can be expensive, but it really is worth using the best you can afford. Even when you are pickling fruit, or making warm spicy chutneys or tomato ketchup, please don't skimp. The final taste of any dish can only be as good as the ingredients that have gone into its creation.

Bruschetta with aged balsamic vinegar

We serve this at the restaurant occasionally as something to nibble on with an aperitif. It is very simple, but delicious – a lovely way to showcase the beautiful rich depth of a *balsamico tradizionale*. I like to use a peasant-style bread without salt, such as pane toscano, pagnotta pugliese or a good-quality ciabatta. I prefer to sprinkle the salt on myself once the bread is toasted, lightly rubbed with garlic, doused with olive oil and finished off with just a trickle of balsamic vinegar.

Serves 4

4 slices of good-quality chewy, peasant-style bread, cut about 1cm thick

1 garlic clove, peeled

2 tbsp good-quality mild-tasting extra virgin olive oil

4 tsp aged balsamic vinegar

good pinch of sea salt

a little finely chopped parsley, to finish (optional)

Preheat your grill and toast the slices of bread until golden on both sides. Remove from the grill and, while still warm, rub gently all over with the garlic clove. Cut the slices in half and brush with the olive oil.

Drizzle over the balsamic vinegar and sprinkle with sea salt and a little chopped parsley if you like. Serve at once, while still warm. Delicious with a glass of Prosecco…

Pickled pumpkin with burrata

This pairing of sweet, sharp pickled pumpkin slices with burrata – a gentle, creamy, rich, cow's milk mozzarella from Puglia in Italy – makes a delectable first course. You'll have more pickled pumpkin than you need here, but it is worth making a reasonable quantity because it is lovely with so many things. Try it with slow-cooked veal; or smoked eel topped with a dollop of crème fraîche, laced with grated horseradish; or chopped and tossed through a salad of lentils and warm chorizo.

Serves 4

Pickled pumpkin

1 small flavourful pumpkin, or onion or butternut squash, about 1.5–2kg

220g caster sugar

200ml good-quality red wine vinegar

1 bottle (750ml) verjuice or white wine

3 bay leaves

2 tsp coriander seeds

1 tsp fennel seeds

small bunch of lemon thyme (or regular thyme)

1 red chilli

Salad

small bunch of marjoram or oregano, leaves only

sea salt and freshly ground black pepper

few drops of lemon juice

50–60ml extra virgin olive oil

12 slices of pickled pumpkin

8 slow-roasted tomato halves (see page 123)

1 burrata or buffalo mozzarella

4 tsp aged balsamic vinegar

For the pickled pumpkin, put all the ingredients except the pumpkin into a heavy-based wide pan. Place over a low heat to allow the sugar to dissolve, stirring once or twice, then turn up the heat slightly to encourage the flavours to merge and get to know one another. Meanwhile, cut the pumpkin in half and scoop out the seeds, but leave the skin on. Slice the pumpkin into long fine wedges – the slices need to be thin to allow the sweet pickling flavour to permeate right through.

Place the pumpkin slices in the simmering pickling liquid. Turn the heat down as low as possible and poach very gently for 45 minutes until the pumpkin is tender to the bite – it should taste sweet and sour. Allow to cool in the syrup, then lift out the pickled pumpkin slices and pack into sterilised jars. Strain the pickling liquor and pour over the pumpkin. Seal and store in a cool dark place or the fridge – it will last a good few weeks.

For the salad, using a pestle and mortar, gently pound the herb leaves with a small pinch of salt to a rough paste. Sprinkle over the lemon juice, add the extra virgin olive oil and stir well to combine. Taste the dressing for seasoning, adding a little pepper.

Arrange the pumpkin slices and slow-roasted tomatoes on serving plates and spoon the burrata or tear the mozzarella on top. Drizzle the herb dressing over the salad and around the plate. Trickle over the balsamic vinegar and serve.

The pumpkin I use for this recipe is the thin grey-skinned variety called Queensland blue, which has a pleasing texture when cooked. Onion and butternut squash work well too.

Pan-fried mackerel with red wine vinegar, horseradish and crème fraîche

Mackerel is a beautiful rich, oily fish that needs to be eaten very fresh to be fully enjoyed. The sharpness of the vinegar helps to cut the richness and the heat of the horseradish and soft, sweet-sour flavour of crème fraîche make this a lovely dish. Serve it with some little warm potatoes that have been dressed with olive oil and sprinkled with chopped flat leaf parsley, or, as I do in the summer, with a bowl of green beans.

Serves 4

4 medium or 8 small mackerel, cleaned, and filleted if preferred

3 tbsp olive oil

sea salt and freshly ground black pepper

Sauce

4cm piece of fresh horseradish

2 tbsp red wine vinegar

220ml crème fraîche

When you are cooking fish,

avoid overcrowding the pan. Either cook the fish in batches or use two pans.

Start by making the sauce. Peel the horseradish and grate it as finely as possible. (Be careful though, as very fresh horseradish will make you cry!) Tip the grated horseradish into a bowl and pour on the wine vinegar. Stir well to combine. Fold in the crème fraîche and season generously with salt, but only the smallest pinch of pepper. Set aside while you cook the fish.

If leaving the fish whole, rinse the cavity and pat dry. Using a sharp knife, make 3 diagonal slits on both sides of each fish. Brush the fish with a little olive oil and season with salt and pepper. Heat a large pan over a high heat. If you are cooking the fish filleted, season the skin side only and pour the oil into the pan rather than rub it over the fish.

When the pan is hot, lay the fish in the pan – fillets should be placed skin side down. Cook whole fish without moving for 3 minutes on one side, then turn the fish over and cook on the other side for 3 minutes. Cook fillets for 4 minutes only without turning – just allow the flesh to cook through the skin side, for a more delicate texture. The skin should have turned from silver to almost bronze and be papery thin and just crisp.

Arrange the fish on warm plates. Spoon the horseradish sauce alongside and serve piping hot – the best way to enjoy oily fish.

Slow-cooked shoulder of lamb with red wine vinegar

Shoulder of lamb cooked in this way becomes meltingly soft and tender. The shoulder contains more fat than the leg, which gives the meat a sweeter, fuller flavour. Red wine vinegar helps to cut the richness, while giving the dish a deep, sharp, yet mellow note. The addition of anchovy is a lovely way to add saltiness to slow-cooked dishes.

Serves 4–6

1 shoulder of lamb, bone in, about 1.5–2kg

sea salt and freshly ground black pepper

1 tbsp olive oil

3/4 bottle (about 560ml) white wine

1 tsp fennel seeds

2 dried red chillies, roughly chopped

5 garlic cloves, peeled

bunch of sage

1 bay leaf

6 good-quality anchovy fillets, packed in oil

5 tbsp red wine vinegar

I add dried red chilli early

on to many slow-cooked dishes, as it provides a warm undertone, lending a profoundly satisfying flavour. In contrast to fresh chillies, which give unquestionable heat to dishes, dried chillies provide only warmth.

Preheat the oven to 160°C/Gas 3. Using a small sharp knife, trim the lamb of most of its surface fat, then season the meat liberally all over. Place a large frying pan (big enough to hold the lamb shoulder) on the hob over a medium heat. Add the olive oil and when the pan is really hot, put in the lamb shoulder. Brown the meat well on all sides, turning as necessary; it will take about 10 minutes to achieve a good colour all over.

Transfer the meat to a roasting tray and pour off the fat from the pan. Return the pan to a low heat and pour in the wine. Let it bubble and reduce for a couple of minutes, then pour over the lamb.

Toast the fennel seeds in a dry pan until fragrant. Add to the roasting tray along with the chopped chillies, whole garlic cloves, sage, bay leaf, anchovies and wine vinegar. Cover the pan with foil, sealing it tightly around the edges. Cook on the middle shelf of the oven for 3 hours.

Take the lamb out of the oven and remove the foil. Return to the oven and cook for a further 30 minutes, by which stage the meat should be very soft and wonderfully brown. Taste the sauce for seasoning and adjust if necessary – it should be mellow, but rich and satisfying in flavour. I often serve this dish with farro or little white beans, but potatoes would be good too.

Garlic

*I find that almost everyone is seduced by the sweet smell
of garlic cooking. As it emanates from the kitchen, the
aroma draws you in, making you feel hungry. It is perhaps
the most alluring of all smells, but to describe it is almost
impossible. It is pungent, earthy and powerful most
certainly, but also subtle and delicate...*

*Garlic has been grown since time immemorial and has a
place in almost all civilisations -- ancient as well as modern
– in culinary, medicinal and religious contexts. Varieties
range from the smaller purple-tinged Italian and Spanish
bulbs to big elephant garlic, which is very mild.*

*We tend to associate garlic with strength and punch, but
it can be used delicately in dishes, too. Generally, the more
garlic is pounded or chopped, the stronger the taste.
I rarely add garlic at the start of cooking, preferring to add it
later – sometimes halfway through – but certainly after
base flavouring ingredients such as onions, celery and
carrots. The result is a fuller, softer, more satisfying flavour.*

Garlic is harvested in late spring and early summer. I always look forward to new season's spring garlic, with its long green stalk and lovely rose-tinged creamy bulb, all encased in fine, papery, ivory skin. At this time of year, the individual cloves are not yet fully formed, and the immature papery layers in between them are completely edible. I like to braise the soft heads whole in stock or wine to enjoy their sweet, tender flesh.

Garlic can also be grown at home. Try planting a single clove (or a handful) in your garden in the autumn, and come spring – if you are lucky – young green shoots will begin to appear. These shoots are good to eat too – lightly sautéed or added to salads.

◊

Wild garlic, which is also available in the spring, is quite different. It has fragrant, long, flat dark green leaves, but no bulb. You'll most likely come across it in damp woodlands or along riverbanks. Look out for bluebells – the chances are wild garlic will be growing alongside. I simply wash the leaves and toss them quickly in a pan with a little oil or butter to serve alongside lamb, or with the first of the season's wild salmon.

◊

When buying garlic, search out bulbs that are tight, firm and hard, without any discolouration or bruises. If you've ever eaten a clove that is discoloured and soft, you will not have forgotten its rancid taste and smell. Damaged cloves can spoil the taste of a cooked dish, so be sure to discard them. Store garlic bulbs in a cool, dry place, with good air circulation (not the fridge). Do not use garlic that has developed small green shoots. Also, if garlic is to be eaten raw, the central green shoot running through the middle of the clove should be removed, as it is indigestible.

◊

Aïoli is a pungent, garlicky sauce – delicious served alongside simply poached fish or grilled shellfish, or stirred into seafood stews at the last minute. It is also lovely with raw tender young vegetables, or a salad of sliced ripe tomatoes and green beans.

Aïoli My version is more gentle than the classic rustic Provençal sauce prepared from stale bread, garlic and olive oil. To make it, pound 6 peeled garlic gloves to a paste with 1/2 tsp salt, using a pestle and mortar. In a bowl, lightly beat 2 organic free-range egg yolks with the pounded garlic and the juice of 1/2 lemon to combine. Measure 250ml Provençal or other mild-tasting extra virgin olive oil. Slowly begin to incorporate the oil into the garlicky base, drip by drip to begin, whisking all the time. As the sauce begins to emulsify, you can add the oil a little more quickly. When it is all added, you should have a lovely thick garlicky mayonnaise – aïoli!

Baked garlic and shallots with fino

I make this dish in the spring, when the new season's garlic arrives. Its soft cloves – encased in sweet papery casings – are gentle in flavour, and the heads can be roasted and eaten whole. They go beautifully with roasted shallots. Serve as I do, on grilled bread, with a spoonful or two of spring goat's curd, or as an accompaniment to simple roast chicken.

Serves 4

4 heads of new season's garlic

8 banana shallots

sea salt and freshly ground black pepper

5 lemon thyme sprigs (or ordinary thyme)

4 bay leaves

600ml fresh chicken stock

180ml fino sherry

50g unsalted butter, in pieces

50g Parmesan, freshly grated

Preheat the oven to 180°C/Gas 4. Slice the garlic heads in half horizontally and place in a roasting tray. Halve the shallots and slip off their outer skin. Add to the garlic, season with salt and pepper, and scatter over the thyme and bay. Bring the chicken stock to the boil in a small pan, then pour over the garlic and shallots. Drizzle over the sherry.

Cover the tray tightly with foil and roast in the oven for 40 minutes. Remove the foil and return to the oven for a further 15 minutes until the shallots and garlic are golden brown and the stock has reduced down and thickened. Add the butter and Parmesan and stir to combine. Taste and adjust the seasoning, then serve.

Fried egg with sage, chilli and garlicky yoghurt

The combination of garlic, yoghurt and olive oil is compulsive. I use it not only for this dish, but also with perfectly ripe sweet tomatoes; with grated cucumber to make tzatziki; with roasted chicken; or simply on toast. You could poach the eggs if you prefer, but I think the crispy bits of the fried egg taste particularly good with the brown butter and creamy yoghurt.

Serves 4

240ml good-quality Greek-style yoghurt (thick and only mildly sharp)

2 garlic cloves, peeled and crushed

sea salt

50ml extra virgin olive oil

80g unsalted butter

8 sage leaves

4 very fresh organic free-range eggs

1 red chilli, very finely sliced into rings (seeds left in)

Put the yoghurt into a bowl with the garlic, a good pinch of salt and the extra virgin olive oil. Stir well to combine, taste and add a little more salt if necessary. Set aside to allow the flavours to adjust to each other while you brown the butter.

Place the butter in a non-stick pan along with the sage leaves over a medium heat. Cook, stirring gently, until the butter begins to separate firstly, and then brown. The sediment at the bottom will taste nutty and delicious. You can strain it to remove the sediment if you like, but I prefer to leave it in. Set aside in a warm place while you cook the eggs.

Place one large (or two) non-stick frying pan(s) over a medium heat. Add a teaspoon of the browned butter, without the nutty sediment, to each pan. When hot, crack the eggs into the pans and add the sliced chilli. Cook until the whites are firm and the yolks are soft. I like to spoon the hot butter over the whites to encourage the eggs to cook more quickly and to flavour them.

To serve, divide the garlicky yoghurt among four plates, carefully lay the eggs on top and scatter over the chilli. Spoon the warm sage butter over the eggs and serve at once.

Very fresh eggs have bright, shiny yolks that sit proudly on top of bouncy, thick whites as you crack them into the pan. Thin, runny whites are an indication that the eggs are less than fresh.

Chicken with garlic and fennel

This is the sort of food I cook at home – quick, simple and satisfying. During the summer, I'll most likely serve it with a plate of green beans and new potatoes from the garden, drizzled with peppery extra virgin olive oil.

Serves 4

1 organic free-range chicken, about 1.4kg, jointed into 8 pieces

sea salt and freshly ground black pepper

2 tbsp olive oil

1 tsp fennel seeds

1 tsp coriander seeds

2 red onions, peeled and finely sliced

1 dried red chilli

1 tsp saffron threads

4 garlic cloves, peeled and crushed

2 fennel bulbs, trimmed and fibrous outer layer removed

250ml white wine

2 x 340g jars (or tinned) good-quality peeled plum tomatoes

pared zest of 1 orange

3 bay leaves

5 thyme sprigs

1–2 tbsp extra virgin olive oil (optional)

Season the chicken well all over with salt and pepper. Put the olive oil into a flameproof casserole (large enough to hold all the ingredients comfortably) and place over a medium heat. When hot, brown the chicken pieces in batches, turning to colour them all over – they should look really golden and pleasing to the eye. Once browned, remove the pieces and set aside. Pour off any excess fat from the casserole, leaving around 1 tbsp or so.

In a separate pan, gently warm the fennel and coriander seeds until they release their fragrance, then tip into a mortar and pound with the pestle to grind finely.

Add the onions to the casserole and cook over a low heat until sweet and translucent, about 5 minutes. Crumble over the chilli and add the ground spices, saffron and garlic. Season with a good pinch of salt and a little pepper, and stir well to combine. Cut the fennel bulb into quarters and add to the pan.

Pour in the wine, turn up the heat a little and let bubble and reduce for a minute or so, then add the tomatoes. Return the chicken to the pan and add the orange zest and herbs. Turn the heat down and put the lid on the casserole. Cook very gently for 40 minutes or until the chicken is cooked through and almost starting to fall from the bone.

Taste and adjust the seasoning. If you're like me, you'll want to add a splash of extra virgin olive oil to bring the whole dish together. Serve with bread – or something else to mop up the delicious juices.

A dish such as this often tastes even better if allowed to cool to room temperature before reheating to serve. The flavours somehow adjust, get to know each other and are that much better for it.

Good-quality pork is **essential** for this dish. We use a variety of pig known as Middlewhite, which is small in stature with sweet flesh – particularly that of the female. Male flesh invariably tastes a little stronger.

Slow-roasted pork belly with sprouting broccoli and puréed garlic

I love the creamy, smooth and ever-so-slightly-pungent garlic purée that you find in Middle Eastern restaurants. Having never managed to persuade anyone to give me the recipe I decided to come up with my own. It's really not bad and goes beautifully with the sweet, succulent flesh of pork belly. I find the crunchy crackling – achieved by cooking the pork in this way – totally irresistible.

Serves 6–8

2kg pork belly, with skin on and ribs intact

50ml olive oil

sea salt and freshly ground black pepper

1 tbsp fennel seeds

4 carrots, peeled and cut into chunks

4 celery sticks, cut into chunks

2 red onions, peeled and roughly chopped

3 bay leaves

few rosemary sprigs

2 dried red chillies

500ml white wine

Garlic purée

20 very fresh garlic cloves, peeled but left whole

200ml whole milk

3 lemon thyme (or ordinary thyme) sprigs

50ml mild-tasting extra virgin olive oil

few drops of lemon juice

Sprouting broccoli

750g sprouting broccoli, trimmed

40ml extra virgin olive oil

1 red chilli, sliced (optional)

Preheat the oven to 200°C/Gas 6. Using a very sharp knife, score the skin of the pork at regular intervals, making the cuts about 5mm deep. Rub the olive oil into the flesh and season well all over with 1 tbsp sea salt and the fennel seeds. Place the pork belly, skin side up, in a roasting tray and roast on the middle shelf of the oven for 45 minutes until the skin begins to blister and colour, and the crackling begins to form.

Carefully lift out the pork onto a platter and scatter the vegetables, herbs and dried chillies in the roasting tray. Pour over the wine, season lightly and stir to combine. Rest the pork on top of the vegetables and cover with foil. Lower the oven setting to 160°C/ Gas 3. Return the pork to the oven and cook for a further 2 hours. By this time the meat should be meltingly tender. Remove the foil and cook, uncovered for a further 20 minutes.

While the pork is roasting, make the garlic purée. Put the garlic, milk and thyme sprigs in a small saucepan over a gentle heat. Add a pinch of salt and bring to just under a simmer, then turn down the heat to very low and poach the garlic very gently until soft, about 35 minutes. The garlic should be very soft and almost falling apart. Using a slotted spoon, transfer the garlic cloves to a bowl and add a tablespoonful or so of the milk. Mash, using a fork, to a purée, then stir in the olive oil. Add a few drops of lemon juice and season with a little more salt and pepper to taste; keep warm.

When the pork is ready, set aside to rest while you cook the broccoli. Add to a pan of boiling salted water and cook for about 3 minutes. Drain and immediately dress with the extra virgin olive oil and chilli slices if using.

Cut the pork into 2–3cm thick slices, sliding out the bones as you do so and discarding the vegetables. Arrange on warm plates with the broccoli. Spoon over the garlic purée and serve.

Stracotto

Known as *stracotto* in Tuscany, *brasato* in Piedmont, this delectable, melt-in-the-mouth dish is soft enough to eat with a spoon. I cook it every year, when the weather turns cooler and my thoughts turn to food that will nourish and sustain me. Rich and simple, this dish is the sum of its parts – good wine, a good but not expensive cut of meat, some aromatic herbs and patience – the most invaluable ingredient of all. It will take all day to cook … but then good things come to those who wait.

Serves 6

1.5–2kg piece of shoulder or rump of beef, trimmed of most (but not all) of its fat

sea salt and freshly ground black pepper

40ml olive oil

3 yellow onions, peeled and chopped

4 carrots, peeled and roughly chopped

4 celery sticks, trimmed and chopped

10 garlic cloves, peeled but left whole

sprig of bay leaves (4–6 leaves)

small bunch of thyme sprigs

small bunch of flat leaf parsley

1 litre good-quality chicken stock

1 bottle (750ml) red wine, preferably Chianti or Barbaresco

1 pig's trotter (optional)

Season the meat generously all over with salt and pepper, then form into a neat roll and tie with string.

Heat the olive oil in a flameproof casserole (large enough to hold all the ingredients comfortably) over a medium-high heat. When it is hot, add the meat and brown well all over, turning as necessary; this will take about 15 minutes. Lift out onto a plate and set aside.

Now add the vegetables to the casserole with the garlic and herbs, and turn down the heat slightly. Cook over a fairly low heat for 15 minutes until the vegetables are soft and sweet.

Return the meat to the casserole, pour over the stock and wine, and add the pig's trotter if using. Put the lid on and reduce the heat to low. Cook over a very low heat (use a heat diffuser if possible) for 5 hours. Take out the meat and bay leaves, then strain the sauce through a colander, pressing firmly with the back of a ladle to pass the vegetables through – this will thicken and enrich the final sauce.

Return the meat and bay leaves to the pan and pour over the strained sauce. Cook over a very low heat for a further hour. At this point, turn off the heat and allow to cool. (The flavour will be improved if the dish is allowed to come to room temperature and reheated to serve.)

Before serving, reheat the *stracotto* gently – the meat should now be falling apart, with a rich, glossy sauce to accompany it. Serve in warm soup plates, with whatever you like. We sometimes serve it with course yellow polenta, or cavolo nero, or just a salad of winter leaves and good bread with which to mop up the juices.

Game

Feathered game, in all its manifestations, tastes of the
land on which it lived and fed. It has a mossy, woodland
flavour with all the complexities that the particular
landscape offers, but it is also majestic and glorious.
I associate game strongly with England and, more
broadly, Europe. It reminds me of fresh air, sport, a big
hunger and deep robust red wines. Without doubt, it
becomes very much central stage in any dish.

The beauty of game is that each variety has a unique,
deep and satisfying flavour, providing nuances of taste
that are not found in other meats – the delicate slightly
livery taste of pigeon, for example, or the musty earthy
taste of grouse. Game works beautifully with autumn's
bounty of produce – wild mushrooms, root vegetables,
nuts, Brussels sprouts and other brassicas, delicate
cauliflower purée, even pomegranates and quince. Game
offers so many possibilities that I'm always eager for the
start of the season towards the middle of August, when
the first grouse appear.

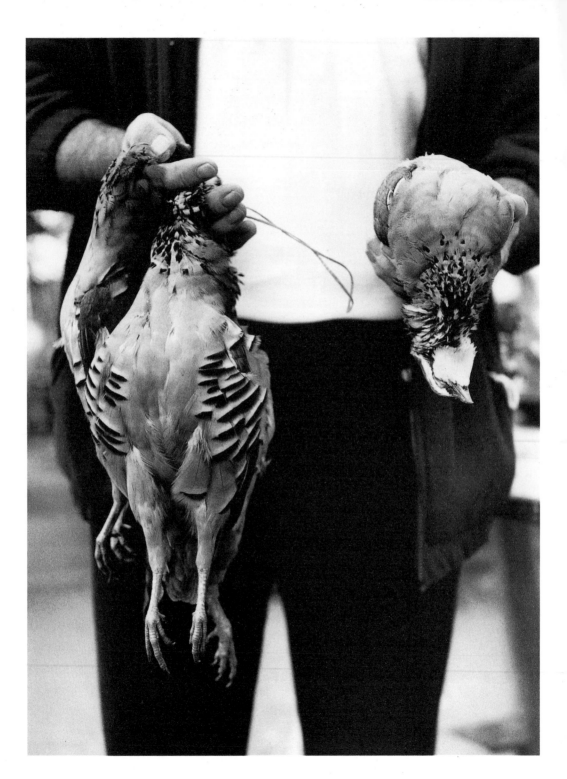

Careful thought and consideration is needed when pairing game with other ingredients. Understandably, bread very often features – in the form of breadcrumbs or bread sauce – as it provides a foil for game meats that have a very strong taste. Grouse, perhaps the most intensely flavoured of all the birds, certainly benefits from this coupling and I often serve it on toast. All game, though very different in taste, has a sense of woodland about it – moss, berries, mushrooms etc. – so these flavours also complement the birds in cooking. The delicate, earthy characteristics of girolles and porcini, for example, work well with partridge, mallard and quail.

Strictly speaking, quail and guinea fowl are classified as poultry rather than game these days, as they are now protected species. Those that you buy will have been farmed, hence their milder taste. As with chicken, seek out free-range birds for optimum flavour.

◊

Game often has a dark appearance and a very strong smell because it has been hung, but you need to be assured that it is in good condition for eating. The fat should be creamy and fairly intact, and the aroma should be decent, albeit strong. Always check game birds for shot too, as the resulting damage can give the meat a taste of metal. Also, torn flesh can dry and harden around the edges – cooking will not improve or mask this damage.

I strongly recommend that you look for a reputable game dealer or butcher, who deals with small hunters and suppliers. Our game dealer, Albert, or 'Albert the Grouseman' as we call him, has dealt in game for many years and always brings us only the very best of what he can lay his hands on. A one-man band, he only ever 'sees what he can do' and his produce never disappoints.

Like Albert, I believe it is best to wait until there is something really good and worthy of cooking than to eat game in less than perfect condition. Our game arrives plucked, hung and ready to eat. We give it a quick wipe over with a clean damp cloth and place it in a sealed large plastic container with space and air surrounding it, then store it in the fridge and cook within a few days of purchase.

Never has nature seemed more noble or majestic than in the lay of the feathers of game birds. Soft like velvet, with both vibrant and muted hues – of amber, rust, chocolate and blue – man could not have created anything quite like this beauty.

Guinea fowl supremes with braised tardivo and balsamic mayonnaise

I am very fond of guinea fowl as it has a gentle taste – no more intense than properly flavoured chicken – and because it was one of my father's favourite things to eat, so it always reminds me of him. Like radicchio, tardivo is delicious grilled, turning bittersweet as it slightly chars – this flavour works well with all game birds. The mayonnaise accompanying the dish is caramely, rich and elegant; it complements the tender meat perfectly.

Serves 4

1 large head of tardivo or radicchio

4 tbsp extra virgin olive oil

sea salt and freshly ground black pepper

3 tbsp aged balsamic vinegar

4 guinea fowl supremes (breasts with the wing tip attached)

1–2 tbsp olive oil, for frying

Balsamic mayonnaise

3 organic free-range egg yolks

1/2 tbsp Dijon mustard

1 tbsp lemon juice

250ml mild-tasting extra virgin olive oil

2 tbsp aged balsamic vinegar

First make the mayonnaise. Whisk the egg yolks with a pinch of salt, then whisk in the mustard and lemon juice. Trickle in the olive oil, very slowly to begin with, whisking constantly, then more steadily once the sauce begins to emulsify. Continue until all the oil is incorporated. Stir in the balsamic vinegar and set aside to let the flavours become acquainted, while you cook the dish.

Preheat the oven to 220°C/Gas 7 and heat the grill. To prepare the tardivo or radicchio, remove any wilted or damaged leaves, then slice vertically into 4cm wedges so that the leaves are still attached to the core. Toss in a bowl with the extra virgin olive oil to coat and season with salt. Allow to stand for a minute or two, to allow the oil to soften the leaves slightly.

Place the tardivo cut side down on the grill rack and cook until slightly charred at the edges. Turn and cook for about 3 minutes on the other side. Don't be tempted to prod it during cooking; as the outer leaves char, the inner ones will soften, becoming sweet and tender. Dress while still warm with the balsamic vinegar.

To cook the guinea fowl, season generously on both sides with salt and pepper. Place a large heavy-based frying pan (suitable for use in the oven and preferably non-stick) over a fairly high heat. When the pan is smoking hot, add the olive oil, then brown the guinea fowl in batches. Lay 2 supremes in the pan, skin side down, and cook without moving for about 3 minutes. Remove to a warm plate and repeat with the other 2 supremes, adding a little more oil if needed.

Return the first 2 supremes to the pan, skin side down, then place the pan in the oven for about 8 minutes to finish cooking the guinea fowl – the skin will be very crisp and the flesh should be firm, succulent and tender. Set aside to rest for 5 minutes.

Warm the tardivo if necessary and serve with the guinea fowl. Hand round the mayonnaise separately so everyone can help themselves.

Grilled partridge with chilli, marjoram and ricotta

This is a slightly surprising, but delicious way to treat partridge. Instead of pairing it in the usual manner with rich wine, nuts, mushrooms or bread, here it is spiked with the clean, vibrant flavours of marjoram, chilli and lemon juice. This works particularly well with the slightly charred succulence of meat that has been cooked over an open fire. Very fresh sheep's milk ricotta rounds the dish off with a delicate sweetness.

Serves 4

4 grey-legged partridges, plucked and cleaned, but not trussed

sea salt and freshly ground black pepper

2 red chillies, finely sliced

handful of marjoram sprigs, plus extra leaves to finish

1 lemon, halved

5 tbsp very good extra virgin olive oil

8 thin slices of pancetta

4 slices of crusty, white peasant-style bread

200g very fresh sheep's milk ricotta

lemon wedges, to serve

Using poultry scissors, cut away the backbone of each partridge, to enable you to open the bird out. The easiest way is to do this is to cut either side of the bone where the ribs join, then push the bird out flat with your open hand.

Put the birds into a large shallow dish. Season them with salt and pepper, and scatter over the sliced chillies and marjoram. Squeeze over the lemon juice and drizzle with all but 1 tbsp of the extra virgin olive oil. Turn the birds to coat once or twice, then leave to marinate for 30 minutes or so.

Heat up your barbecue or preheat the grill or griddle pan. When hot, lay the partridges skin side down on the rack or griddle. Cook, turning frequently so that they brown and cook evenly all over, for about 25 minutes until the flesh is pink and tender, but not too rare. Remove the partridges to a warm plate and rest for 5 minutes.

In the meantime, cook the pancetta slices and toast the bread on the barbecue or griddle. Place a slice of toast on each warm plate and drizzle with a little olive oil. Add a spoonful of ricotta and a slice of pancetta, then a scattering of marjoram. Place a partridge on top and serve at once, with lemon wedges.

Grey-legged partridges are more delicious than their red-legged cousins in my view. Like other game, an early salting will improve the juiciness and texture of these little birds and give time for the seasoning to diffuse through the meat. Allow 1 tbsp of good-quality sea salt to each bird. Salt evenly all over and refrigerate for at least 24 hours. Wipe off any excess salt and do not re-season before cooking.

Mallard with porcini and red wine

With the exception of confit, which I love to eat in the winter, I don't cook duck all that often. Duck breast, cooked in the usual way, does little for me. However, the young wild ducks that are around in the autumn and early winter are altogether different. Small enough for one, their rich, tender flesh is lovely. Here I've matched them with fresh porcini and a simple red wine reduction. You might like to serve them with soft polenta. *Illustrated on previous page*

Serves 4

4 small, young mallards, plucked and cleaned

120g unsalted butter

sea salt and freshly ground black pepper

250g fresh porcini mushrooms (if unavailable use 50g dried porcini)

1 bottle (750ml) good-quality red wine

few rosemary sprigs

1 garlic clove, peeled and crushed

Preheat the oven to 200°C/Gas 6. Wash the mallards and pat dry. Now spatchcock them: cut down either side of the backbone, then open the birds out and press down with the heel of your hand to flatten. Smear a small knob of butter over the breast of each bird (use two-thirds of the butter) and season generously all over.

To prepare the fresh porcini, carefully scrape away any dirt with a sharp bendy knife, then wipe them over with a damp cloth. Cut them in half lengthways and check there are no worms. Remove any damaged bases from the caps, but do not discard them. (If using dried porcini, soak in hot water for about 15 minutes. Remove the mushrooms and set aside; strain the liquor through a fine sieve.)

Pour the red wine into a wide saucepan and add the rosemary sprigs and trimmed mushroom bases (or reserved soaking liquor). Bring to a simmer over a medium heat and let bubble until reduced by almost half; strain and set aside.

Place the little ducks in a roasting tray, but don't overcrowd the pan (use two trays if necessary). Place on the middle shelf of the oven and roast for about 20 minutes, basting halfway through cooking. This timing will give you beautifully cooked birds, but you can always allow a few minutes longer if you like, or a few minutes less if you prefer the meat rare. Set aside in a warm place to rest while you cook the porcini.

Place a non-stick frying pan over a medium-high heat and add the remaining 40g butter. When it is foaming, throw in the porcini and garlic, and season with a little salt and pepper. Cook undisturbed for a minute, then turn and cook on the other side for a couple of minutes. The porcini should have taken on a wonderful colour around the edges. Pour in the reduced wine and cook for a further 5 minutes.

Place a mallard on each warm plate and spoon the porcini and sauce over. Serve at once.

Roasted quail with girolles and spinach

Delicate little quail may offer you no more than five or six mouthfuls each, but their flesh has such a delightful sweet, nutty flavour that I adore eating them. Girolle mushrooms – pan-fried with a little garlic and tossed through with velvety small spinach leaves – make a wonderful and natural partner.

Serves 4

8 quails

200g girolles or chanterelles

500g young spinach leaves (or pousse)

100g unsalted butter

sea salt and freshly ground black pepper

1 garlic clove, peeled and finely chopped

generous squeeze of lemon juice, to taste

Preheat the oven to 200°C/Gas 6. Wash the quails and pat dry. Wipe the mushrooms with a clean, soft, damp cloth to remove any dirt (never rinse them, as you will wash away their gentle flavour). Wash the spinach thoroughly under cold running water, then drain in a colander.

Place a small knob of butter inside the cavity of each bird, then smear a little over the breast (to use about half of the butter). Season generously with salt and pepper. Place the quails in a roasting pan on the middle shelf of the oven and roast for about 12–15 minutes until the breast is firm to the touch.

While the quail is cooking, cook the spinach in batches if necessary. Simply place it in a dry pan with only the water clinging to the leaves after washing and cook briefly over a medium heat until just wilted. Drain in a colander and leave until cool enough to handle, then squeeze with your hands to remove excess water and set aside while you cook the mushrooms. Once the quail are cooked, set them aside to rest in a warm place.

To cook the mushrooms, place a non-stick frying pan over a fairly high heat. Once the pan is hot, add a third of the remaining butter and allow it to sizzle slightly, then add the girolles and season lightly with salt and pepper. Leave to cook for a couple of minutes – don't prod or poke them as this encourages them to release moisture and can ruin their final texture.

Now add the garlic and spinach to the mushrooms and stir to heat the spinach and mingle the flavours. Add the rest of the butter, a good squeeze of lemon juice and a grinding of black pepper.

Serve the spinach and mushrooms piping hot alongside the quail. I strongly recommend this dish ... I think it is really lovely.

Pigeon with borlotti and cavolo

In this recipe I have used dried borlotti beans, which are different from the beautiful fresh borlotti beans we grow in our vegetable garden in the summer. The dried beans are heavier and less creamy, but delicious with cavolo nero – and perfect with roasted pigeon.

Serves 4

4 squab (young pigeons), plucked and cleaned, but not trussed

olive oil, to drizzle

sea salt and freshly ground black pepper

Borlotti beans

450g dried borlotti beans, soaked overnight

340g jar (or tinned) good-quality peeled plum tomatoes, chopped

1 small bunch of sage

1 head of garlic, halved crossways

1 dried red chilli

120ml extra virgin olive oil

Cavolo nero

500g cavolo nero

about 40ml extra virgin olive oil

50g unsalted butter

2 garlic cloves, peeled and finely chopped

4 good-quality tinned anchovy fillets in olive oil, drained

1/2 dried red chilli

Drain the borlotti beans and put them into a large heavy-based cooking pot. Cover generously with cold water, but do not season. Add the plum tomatoes, sage and garlic, then crumble over the chilli. Bring to the boil over a medium heat, then turn the heat down and simmer until the beans are tender to the bite; this should take about 45 minutes.

In the meantime, cook the pigeons. Preheat the oven to 230°C/Gas 8. Place the pigeons in a lightly oiled roasting tray, season them well all over and inside the cavity, and drizzle with a little olive oil. Place in the hot oven and roast for 15–20 minutes, depending on size, until tender. When cooked, set aside to rest in a warm place for 10 minutes.

When the borlotti are cooked, season them with a good pinch of salt. Drain and dress while warm with the extra virgin olive oil. Set aside while you cook the cavolo nero.

Bring a large pan of well-salted water to the boil. Wash the cavolo leaves and strip them from their woody central stalks. Once the water is boiling vigorously, plunge in the cavolo leaves and cook for 2–3 minutes until tender to the bite. Drain in a colander and dress with the extra virgin olive oil while warm.

Take half of the cavolo and place it in a blender with the butter, garlic, anchovies and dried chilli. Purée until smooth, adding a little more olive oil if the mixture is too thick – it should be inky black, glossy and smooth. Season to taste with salt and a little pepper.

Return the purée to the pan and stir in the whole cavolo nero leaves and borlotti beans. Warm through and serve piping hot alongside the roasted pigeon.

Roasted grouse with Barolo on toast

The 12th of August marks the beginning of the game season with the appearance of the first small grouse. The ideal size for one, grouse have a particular deep, rich, complex flavour and, when properly cooked, they are perfectly tender. Here I've served them simply with a rich wine sauce, made from Italian Barolo, and crunchy, yet slightly sodden toast... if that makes any sense.

Serves 4

4 grouse, plucked and cleaned, but not trussed

160g unsalted butter

small bunch of thyme

sea salt and freshly ground black pepper

4 slices of chewy peasant-style bread

4 fresh porcini, ceps or field mushrooms, cleaned and thickly sliced

handful of tardivo or roughly torn radicchio leaves

handful of pissenlit (dandelion) or frisée

drizzle of olive oil

few drops of lemon juice

400ml Barolo wine

1 tbsp finely chopped parsley

Preheat the oven to 230°C/Gas 8. Wash the birds and pat dry. Place 20g of the butter in a sturdy flameproof casserole and melt slowly over a gentle heat. Divide the thyme in four and insert a portion into the cavity of each bird. Place a knob of butter inside each bird and smear more butter over the breasts, reserving 60g to cook the porcini and finish the sauce. Season the birds generously with salt and pepper.

Place the grouse in the casserole dish and put on the middle shelf of the oven. Roast for 10 minutes, then remove from the oven and baste in the now-foaming butter.

Place a slice of bread under each grouse and return to the oven for 5 minutes to finish cooking the birds and effectively fry the bread. The bread will not only crisp up, but also absorb all the lovely flavours of the grouse. The skin of the grouse should be crisp and, when pressed with your finger, the flesh should be bouncy and firm.

In the meantime, melt half the remaining butter in a frying pan. When foaming, add the sliced mushrooms and season with a little salt and pepper. Cook, turning occasionally, until tender.

Dress the salad leaves with a little olive oil and lemon juice, and season lightly with salt and pepper.

Transfer the grouse and toast to a warm platter; keep warm. Place the casserole on the hob over a high heat and pour in the wine, stirring to deglaze. Let bubble until reduced by half, swirling the casserole every now and then to gather up all the tasty pan juices.

Arrange the birds on toast on individual plates. Add the final knob of butter to the wine reduction, stirring vigorously as it melts into the sauce. Taste and add a little salt and pepper if required, then spoon over the birds. Pile the salad leaves and mushrooms on top and sprinkle with chopped parsley. Serve at once.

Apples

The English have long loved the cultivation and eating of apples – almost two and a half thousand different varieties have been grown in this country at one time or another. My thoughts always turn to them come early September, though in truth apples are in season here from July until early March. During July and August, like everyone else, I become immersed in the abundance of summer fruit in season – soft ripe berries, cherries, peaches, nectarines and juicy orange-fleshed melons from Italy – anxious not to miss out on any of them. It is without doubt the best time of the year for fruit and so, sadly for apples, I tend to overlook them.

However, as soon as September arrives and the weather gradually begins to turn cooler, I find myself thinking about apples – all the different varieties with their beautiful colours, flavours and textures – and how I can use them in the kitchen.

At one time, orchards in England were as important to the landscape – and to the people who tended them and cooked with their produce – as vineyards are to the French, and olive groves are to the Italians. In essence, they have contributed to England's historical identity. Sadly these days we see few varieties, because supermarkets and most food outlets concentrate on selling those apples that are easiest to grow and have long shelf lives – many flown in from halfway across the world. No longer are beautiful English varieties with intriguing names such as Cox's Orange Pippin, Laxton's Fortune, Cornish Gillyflower and Pitmaston Pine familiar to all.

◊

Each year at Petersham we celebrate Apple Day on 21st October. This year we made toffee apples and old-fashioned tomato and apple ketchup to sell in the café. We also slow-cooked suckling pig and served it warm, wrapped in sourdough bread with apple sauce. Wendy, who I work with, stayed up long into the night to reproduce a Victorian board game, rather like snakes and ladders – for children to play on tables in the café in between bobbing for apples. Brogdale and Chegworth Valley farms in Kent supplied us with rare breed apples to sell by the kilo. As we laid these out on a long table for comparison, the different varieties simply took your breath away – their forms, colours and aromas are so diverse.

◊

A good apple is full of character and its mere appearance can make you smile. I love the individual characters and particular colours of apples. Their imperfections are to be embraced and enjoyed. Of all the varieties, Cox's Orange Pippin is probably the one I use most frequently – in salads and desserts, including baking.

Apples are wonderful combined in salads with autumn nuts, sharp cheeses and gentle sweet lettuces. They are also excellent paired with cabbage, the last of the summer's tomatoes, sweet crab meat or young pork. And, of course, apples lend themselves to all manner of spicy chutneys and jellies, warm tarts and puddings, and refreshing sorbets and ice creams. The possibilities are endless.

When it comes to choosing apples, opt for those that feel firm and heavy for their size. They should be free of blemishes and have a fresh aroma. Try to seek out the more unusual varieties, too. Begin by asking your greengrocer or local farmers' market for particular varieties when they ready for picking. Support local growers who sell a wider range of varieties and, through exploration, discover the myriad and wonderful possibilities of taste that apples can provide.

Apple, fennel, speck and hazelnut salad

This is a crisp, crunchy salad – perfect for late summer or early autumn. The combination of sweet apple, peppery kohlrabi, crunchy fennel and slightly smoky speck is truly delicious. Hazelnuts are a lovely addition, or you could use cobnuts instead when they come into season.

Serves 4

60g hazelnuts

2 Cox's or Russet apples

juice of 1/2 lemon

1 fennel bulb

1 kohlrabi bulb

6 large radicchio leaves

sea salt and freshly ground black pepper

20ml olive oil

8 very thin slices of speck or Parma ham

1 tbsp very finely chopped parsley

Dressing

1 egg yolk

1 tsp Dijon mustard

1 tsp honey

1 tbsp cider vinegar

80ml mild-tasting extra virgin olive oil

2 tsp crème fraîche

Preheat the oven to 180°C/Gas 4. For the dressing, put the egg yolk in a bowl and add the mustard, honey, cider vinegar and some salt and pepper. Whisk to combine, then very slowly pour in the extra virgin olive oil, whisking as you do so, until it is all added and the dressing is combined. Stir in the crème fraîche and set aside.

Scatter the hazelnuts on a roasting tray and lightly toast them in the oven for about 4 minutes. Remove and allow to cool slightly, then rub in a cloth to remove the skins and chop roughly.

For the salad, core the apples and slice into fine discs leaving the skin on. Toss with half of the lemon juice to prevent browning. Remove the tougher outer layer from the fennel and slice into rounds. Peel the kohlrabi and cut into fine discs. Sprinkle the rest of the lemon juice over the fennel and kohlrabi. Wash the radicchio leaves, pat dry and cut into ribbons.

To assemble, put the fennel, kohlrabi, radicchio and apple slices in a bowl. Season with a little salt and pepper and drizzle over the olive oil. Toss together lightly with your fingertips.

Divide the salad among serving plates. Arrange the speck or Parma ham slices on top, drizzle over the dressing and finish with the chopped nuts and parsley. Serve at once.

Kohlrabi, apple and crab salad

Kohlrabi is an underrated vegetable that deserves more recognition. I find its clean, slightly peppery taste irresistible, especially when eaten raw, finely sliced in a salad, perhaps because it is a little like cabbage in flavour. Here it works beautifully with thinly sliced apple and fresh white crab meat.

Serves 4

1 kohlrabi

1 Cox's apple

200g freshly picked white crab meat

handful of curly parsley, stalks removed, leaves finely chopped

30ml extra virgin olive oil

sea salt and freshly ground black pepper

2–3 perfectly ripe tomatoes, sliced

Dressing

1 egg yolk

1¹/2 tsp honey

1 tsp Dijon mustard

1 tbsp cider vinegar

100ml extra virgin olive oil

1 tbsp double cream

Peel the kohlrabi and slice as finely as possible. Core and slice the apple into fine discs leaving the skin on. Place the kohlrabi and apple in a bowl, add the crab meat, chopped parsley and extra virgin olive oil, and season with a little salt and pepper. Toss together lightly with your fingers. Set aside while you make the dressing.

Place the egg yolk in a blender or small food processor and add the honey, mustard, cider vinegar and a little salt and pepper. Whiz to combine then, with the motor running, very slowly drizzle in the olive oil through the feeder tube. When it is all incorporated, add the cream, turn off the motor and pour the dressing into a bowl.

Layer the salad and tomato slices attractively on individual plates, spoon over a little of the dressing and serve right away. Hand the remaining dressing round separately in a jug.

Crab and apple are a delicate combination... sweet and light as air, this salad needs to be dressed with a gentle hand as the flavours require subtlety to be fully appreciated.

Little baked apples

I think of these cheery little apples as comfort food. I love their warmth and caramely, spicy richness. They are simple to make and you needn't be precise with the quantities – adjust the flavourings according to taste, perhaps adding a little chopped candied orange peel as I do.

Serves 4

4 Cox's or Russet apples

8 blanched almonds

2 tbsp apple brandy (or Cognac or ordinary brandy)

1 tbsp currants

1 tbsp sultanas

1 tbsp raisins

finely grated zest and juice of 1 orange

finely grated zest of 1 lemon

3 tbsp muscovado or soft brown sugar

2 tbsp unsalted butter, melted

Jersey cream or vanilla ice cream (see page 34), to serve

Preheat the oven to 180°C/Gas 4. Wash the apples and set aside. Warm the almonds on a baking tray in the oven for a few minutes.

Gently warm the brandy in a small saucepan over a gentle heat. Put the currants, sultanas and raisins in a bowl, add the orange and lemon zest and toss to mix. Pour over the orange juice and the warm brandy, stir to combine and leave for a few minutes to allow the warm alcohol to plump up and soften the dried fruit.

Chop the nuts and add to the mixture with the sugar and melted butter. Stir well, then set aside while you prepare the apples.

Using a small sharp knife, remove a small slice from the base of each apple, so that they will sit happily on a baking tray without rolling over. Hollow out the centre of the apples, making sure that you don't cut right through to the base. Make two little cuts in the skin of each apple – this will help to deter the skin from splitting as the apples swell during cooking.

Spoon the filling into the apples and stand them on a baking tray. Bake on the middle shelf of the oven for 20–25 minutes or until they are tender when pressed and the filling is oozing and bubbling.

Remove from the oven and allow to stand for 5 minutes or so before serving – these little apples taste better served warm rather than piping hot. Hand the cream or ice cream round separately.

Cox's apples are perfect for this recipe. They split and burst slightly in the oven, but their shiny, rosy colour is lovely to behold. Don't use cooking apples – they are too powdery and fall apart.

Apple ice cream with toasted cobnuts and caramel sauce

I love the idea of apple ice cream, but many times I've been disappointed with the outcome, which often seems to taste a little too much like baby food for my liking. Determined to come up with an ice cream that tasted very clearly of apple with a clean, slightly lemony bite, I started experimenting. This is the result...I think it's quite good really.

Serves 4

5 Cox's or Russet apples (or ideally a mixture of the two)

juice of 1 lemon

30ml apple brandy (or Cognac)

150g caster sugar

160ml double cream

Caramel sauce

250g golden caster sugar

125ml water

pinch of sea salt

250ml double cream

To serve

10 cobnuts

Peel, quarter and core the apples, then chop them into small pieces. Put into a blender with the lemon juice and whiz until smooth. Pour in the brandy, add the sugar and blend again. Now pour in the cream and process briefly to combine the mixture. Taste – it should be sweet and boozy, but with a sharp, clean apple finish. Pour into an ice-cream maker and churn until thickened and set, following the manufacturer's instructions.

Preheat the oven to 180°C/Gas 4. Place the cobnuts on a baking tray and roast in the oven for about 6 minutes until golden. Tip onto a board and allow to cool, then chop roughly.

To make the caramel sauce, put the sugar and water into a small heavy-based saucepan over a low heat to dissolve the sugar, stirring once. When dissolved, turn the heat up to medium and cook without stirring to a rich dark caramel – this may take up to 10 minutes.

As the caramel begins to turn golden brown, watch it carefully as it can burn quickly, but take it to a deep mahogany colour (under-cooked caramel tastes insipid). Add the salt and remove from the heat. Immediately pour in the cream – standing well back and protecting your hand with an oven cloth as it tends to splutter. Once it has settled down, return to the heat and cook over a low heat, stirring with a wooden spoon, for a minute or so. Remove from the heat and allow to cool.

To serve, scoop the ice cream into bowls, spoon over a little caramel sauce and sprinkle with the toasted nuts. Serve immediately.

Apple galette

This is a lovely fine apple tart. The pastry is flaky and crunchy and the topping of finely sliced apples is beautifully caramelised. I like to glaze the tart with a special grape jelly that we make in the early autumn from *uva di fragola* (strawberry-scented grapes). It gives the tart the most beautiful purple hue and scented flavour, but you can use apple jelly instead, or simply leave the tart unglazed. This quantity of pastry will make two tarts — it freezes well so I always make enough for another one.

Serves 8

Pastry

500g unbleached plain flour, plus extra to dust

1/2 tsp sea salt

1 tsp caster sugar

375g unsalted butter, cut into 1cm dice

120ml iced water

Apple filling

1kg Cox's or other crisp dessert apples

2 tbsp unsalted butter, melted

180g caster sugar

apple or grape jelly, warmed, to glaze (optional)

Very fine pastry is divine with sweet, fragrant just-cooked apples. Cool, creamy, vanilla ice cream (page 34) that just melts into the warm tart is what is called for here.

To make the pastry, combine the flour, salt and sugar in a large mixing bowl. Add 8 pieces of diced butter and lightly rub into the flour mixture with your fingertips until the mixture resembles coarse sand. Now add the remaining butter dice and work together again lightly with your fingers just until the butter pieces are the size of Smarties. Retaining these large bits of butter makes this pastry really tender.

Now add the iced water in several stages, tossing the mixture together with your fingers until it just comes together. Don't pinch or squeeze the dough or you will overwork it. The amalgamated dough will have some wetter patches and some dryer ones, which is fine. Cut the dough in half and shape each piece firmly into a ball. Wrap each ball tightly in greaseproof paper and flatten with the palm of your hand to a disc, about 2cm thick. Refrigerate for 1 hour. Freeze one portion of dough to use for another tart.

Preheat the oven to 200°C/Gas 6. Unwrap the chilled dough and gently roll out on a lightly floured surface to a 23cm round, 5mm thick. Transfer to a baking tray. Quarter and core the apples, leaving the skin on, then slice thinly – the slices should only be 5mm thick.

Starting about 2.5cm in from the edge of the pastry round, arrange the apples, slightly overlapping, in concentric circles until you reach the centre. Now pinch and twist the edge of the dough, rotating the tart as you do so, to create a border that resembles twisted rope around the apples. Brush the melted butter gently over the apple slices and pastry. Take 2 tbsp of the sugar and sprinkle over the pastry border. Scatter the rest of the sugar over the apples.

Bake in the centre of the oven for about 40 minutes until the apples are soft and the crust is golden brown, rotating the tart 180° after about 15 minutes to ensure it colours evenly. Remove from the oven and allow to rest for 15 minutes, then brush with the warm jelly to glaze if using.

Cheese

*From the beginning I knew that the cheese course would
be important to me at the restaurant, I was also sure that
a large selection would not be right. I've always preferred
to choose from a small, carefully considered menu, rather
than one with endless options. So for the cheese course
one well-chosen cheese – served not with bread or biscuits
but with natural seasonal partners – seemed perfect.
I enjoy the challenge immensely. Finding the right firm,
crunchy, sweet pear (Martin sec) to accompany sharp,
chalky pecorino fossa for example; or autumn raspberries
and a little drizzle of our local honey to partner perfectly
ripe creamy Wigmore. I love the process of tasting a new
cheese ... pausing, thinking, often rejecting, and discussing
with others in the kitchen what works. It is a question of
pairing textures as well as flavours, to showcase the
beauty of not only the cheese, but also its companion.*

Producers and suppliers who have a heartfelt connection with their products, the land and the seasons are of the utmost importance to me. I learn from them and they help me to become a better cook. Patricia Michelson, owner of the Fromagerie, sources farmhouse cheeses directly from small artisan producers. Her energy, passion and knowledge inspire me and her faultless palate always challenges mine!

Cheese, more than any other food, holds a sense of romance for me. It is so much a product of its terrain, flora, fauna and clime, yet its unique attributes are also influenced by man. Some cheeses, like the Swiss vacherin, are purely seasonal; the characteristics of others changes with the seasons. With so many different varieties, there is a myriad of tastes, textures and aromas to experience.

I urge you to find a good cheese shop close to you, peer in through the window and see the magic inside. Try one or two cheeses you may have previously shied away from because their aroma seemed too strong or their names were unpronounceable or off-putting. Stinking bishop, for example, does smell overpowering but it is in fact a delicious complex English cheese.

◊

When choosing cheese, look for signs that it has been respectfully handled. Each cheese is different of course, but there are certain common indicators. The cheese should not look over-handled, neither should it be oily or dry around the edges. Surprisingly, perhaps, mould on the rind of a hard cheese is often a good sign. Above all, a cheese should have a sense of freshness about it.

As for storage, this varies according to the type of cheese. I wrap hard cheeses in cling film, leaving the crust to breathe. Soft cheeses are better wrapped in waxed paper, as are all blue cheeses. Goat's cheeses should be kept loosely covered on a plate in the fridge. Never let cheeses sit uncovered in the fridge – the cold air will dry them out horribly, and their flavour is easily tainted by other foods.

◊

If the idea of serving a very simple cheeseboard of one beautiful cheese with harmonising partners appeals to you, then you might like to try some of the lovely pairings we have stumbled across:
Montgomery's Cheddar with raw fennel and Cox's Orange Pippin.
Vacherin drizzled with the tiniest hint of walnut oil and warmed in the oven along with fresh walnuts (warmed in their shells).
Fourme d'Ambert with dried white figs pickled in red wine.
Young lemony goat's cheeses with ripe apricots and slightly warm pecan nuts.

◊

Using cheese in cooking is another skill. To ensure that a cheese maintains its inherent flavour and texture through the cooking process requires thought and attention. Certain cheeses, including Gruyère, fontina, raclette and Comté, have a natural affinity with heat. Soft young, creamy cheeses work well in baking, but in truth, most cheeses are best enjoyed in their natural state.

Bruschetta of sheep's milk ricotta, lemon oil and bresaola

Light-as-air ricotta is wonderful on grilled bread with thin slices of bresaola – a soft, sweet air-dried cured beef from Italy. This soft sheep's milk cheese is also delicious for breakfast – with a spoonful of honey and perfectly ripe apricots, or summer berries. In winter, I love to flavour it with pounded rosemary and a little dried chilli – to eat with marinated artichokes. It is a truly versatile cheese.

Serves 4

160g sheep's milk ricotta

finely grated zest of 1 lemon

4 slices of good-quality chewy, peasant-style bread, cut about 1cm thick

1 garlic clove, peeled

8 thin slices of bresaola

6 tbsp lemon-infused olive oil (see page 63)

sea salt and freshly ground black pepper

Place the ricotta in a bowl, add the grated lemon zest and fold through gently. Set aside.

Preheat the grill and toast the slices of bread until golden brown on both sides. Once the bread is a really good colour, remove from the grill and rub gently with the garlic clove. Brush the garlicky bread with a little of the lemon-infused oil and season with a little salt.

Arrange a slice of bresaola on each bruschetta on each serving plate. Add a spoonful of ricotta, then top with a final slice of bresaola. Drizzle over a little lemon-infused oil. Finish with a little sprinkling of salt and pepper and serve at once.

For bruschetta, the ideal bread

is an open-pored, well-textured loaf. We use pagnotta, which is baked for us in a wood-fired oven. Ciabatta is another good option.

Aged pecorino with raw sprouts, celery and speck

This salad is all about combining ingredients with good compatible textures and flavours. It has a lovely clean taste. Serve on its own as a starter or with some peasant-style bread for a lunch.

Serves 4

6 Brussels sprouts

180g Parmesan

2–3 celery sticks, washed

20 shelled hazelnuts

1/2 lemon

sea salt and freshly ground black pepper

50ml extra virgin olive oil

12 slices of speck

small handful of curly parsley, leaves only, very finely chopped

Preheat the oven to 180°C/Gas 4. Wash the Brussels sprouts and pat dry. Using a small sharp knife, slice them as finely as you possibly can and place in a bowl. Slice the Parmesan into fine shards, varying the thickness slightly to add interest. Add to the Brussels sprouts. Peel the celery lightly with a swivel vegetable peeler to remove any stringy bits, then cut into shorter lengths and add to the bowl.

Scatter the hazelnuts on a baking tray and warm in the oven for 10 minutes until the nuts are lightly coloured and release their flavour. Let cool slightly, then rub in a cloth to remove the skins. Chop the nuts roughly and set aside.

Squeeze the lemon juice over the salad, season with salt and pepper to taste and drizzle over three-quarters of the extra virgin olive oil. Toss together lightly with your fingers.

Place a slice of speck on each plate and arrange half of the salad over it. Drape another slice of speck on top, then arrange the rest of the salad on top, finishing with a couple of slices of celery and a final slice of Parmesan. Drizzle with the rest of the olive oil and scatter over the hazelnuts. Finish with a sprinkling of chopped parsley.

When buying fresh porcini, look for caps that are firm and dry, not damp in any way. They should smell very fresh – a dank strong smell indicates that they are past their best. Don't keep mushrooms in plastic bags, as they will spoil very easily. Instead store them, loosely covered, in a punnet – preferably in a cool larder rather than the fridge as cold can destroy their delicate flavour.

Wafer-thin slices of porcini with aged Parmesan and crème fraîche

Occasionally through this book you will come across simple salads, comprising no more than two or three ingredients, served raw and finely sliced. At first it might seem surprising to eat mushrooms or asparagus uncooked, in their natural state, but cut as finely as possible, they often taste so much more of their true character to me. Cooking somehow seems to dilute their pure just-picked flavour. *Illustrated on pages 212–3*

Serves 4

200g porcini mushrooms

120g aged Parmesan

1/2 lemon

65ml mild-tasting good-quality extra virgin olive oil

sea salt and freshly ground black pepper

4 tbsp crème fraîche

handful of curly parsley, leaves only, very finely chopped

Wipe the mushrooms carefully and gently with a soft clean cloth or mushroom brush if you have one; don't wash them or the water will soak into the flesh and drown their flavour. Using a small sharp knife, trim the bases, then slice the porcini very finely into wafer-thin slices.

Slice the Parmesan very finely as well. To ensure that the Parmesan does not overpower the perfumed earthy, delicate flavour of the mushrooms, the slices need to be paper-thin.

Toss the sliced porcini and Parmesan together very gently, squeeze over the lemon juice and drizzle with a little of the extra virgin olive oil. Season lightly with salt and pepper – these flavours are too delicate for enthusiastic seasoning. The salad is a whisper of flavours, no more…

Arrange the salad on individual plates, with a spoonful of crème fraîche in the centre. Drizzle over the rest of the olive oil and sprinkle with chopped parsley to serve.

Salad of warm torn bread, poached egg and Parmesan dressing

I love a really good Caesar salad – it just seems hard to find one. This salad – of warm, plump poached fresh eggs, tasty salad leaves, a salty, creamy rich vinaigrette and toast – isn't a Caesar, but its creation came about from a longing for similar flavours. It makes a great brunch or light lunch dish. I vary the leaves and sometimes add slivers of white celery heart. It is the dressing I am most drawn to though ... and the bread with which to mop it up.

Serves 4

12–16 little plum tomatoes, such as San Marzano

sea salt and freshly ground black pepper

60ml mild-tasting extra virgin olive oil

1 or 2 handfuls of mixed leaves, such as mustard leaf, rocket or young spinach

4 slices of good-quality chewy, peasant-style bread, cut about 1cm thick

1 garlic clove, peeled and halved

4 very fresh organic free-range eggs

juice of 1/2 lemon

8 very thin slices of good-quality Parma ham

12–16 shards of Parmesan

Dressing

2 organic free-range egg yolks

1 1/2 tsp English mustard powder

1 garlic clove, peeled

juice of 1 lemon

4 good-quality anchovy fillets in olive oil

60g Parmesan, freshly grated

140ml mild-tasting extra virgin olive oil

1 tbsp crème fraîche

Preheat the oven to 200°C/Gas 6. Pierce the tomatoes with a small knife just once and place on a baking tray. Season with a little salt and pepper and drizzle with a little olive oil. Roast in the oven for 15 minutes or so, until the tomatoes are soft. Remove and allow to cool, reserving the juices.

For the dressing, put the egg yolks, mustard, garlic, lemon juice, anchovies and Parmesan into a blender. With the motor running, very slowly pour in the olive oil through the feeder tube. When all the oil is incorporated, you will have a creamy, slightly thick dressing. Add the crème fraîche and blend briefly to combine. Season generously with pepper, but only a little salt (you may not need any at all). The finished dressing should fall softly from a spoon. If it is too thick, stir in 1 tbsp or so of tepid water.

Place a wide pan of well-salted water on to boil. Wash the salad leaves and pat dry, then place in a bowl.

Preheat the grill and toast the slices of bread until golden brown on both sides, then rub gently with the cut garlic clove. Brush the garlicky bread with a little olive oil and season with a little salt, then cut each slice in half.

Swirl the boiling water in the pan to create a whirlpool, then carefully break in the eggs and poach for 3 minutes. Meanwhile, lightly toss the salad leaves with the rest of the olive oil and the lemon juice, using your fingers. When the eggs are ready, remove and drain on kitchen paper.

To assemble, layer the salad, toast, Parma ham, Parmesan shards and roasted tomatoes on warm individual plates, finishing with a piece of toast. Drizzle over the juice from the cooked tomatoes. Top with the poached egg and spoon over the dressing. Serve at once.

Scallops with rocket, fennel, toasted breadcrumbs and gorgonzola dressing

This combination may seem a little strange, but the flavours are really quite lovely together. The contrast of grilled sweet, plump scallops and a creamy Gorgonzola dressing is seductive and sophisticated. Vary the leaves according to what is available – pissenlit (dandelion) and young spinach (pousse) also work well with these flavours.

Serves 4

20 scallops, shelled and cleaned

1 small head of radicchio

handful of rocket leaves

1 fennel bulb

sea salt and freshly ground black pepper

finely grated zest of 1 lemon

juice of 1/2 lemon

3 tbsp extra virgin olive oil

handful of curly parsley, leaves only, very finely chopped

1 tbsp olive oil

4 tbsp warm toasted sourdough breadcrumbs (see right)

Gorgonzola dressing

1 organic free-range egg yolk

80g Gorgonzola dolce

1 scant tbsp Dijon mustard

1 tbsp sherry vinegar

little squeeze of lemon juice

120ml mild-tasting virgin olive oil

1 tbsp crème fraîche

First make the dressing. Place the egg yolk, Gorgonzola, mustard, sherry vinegar and lemon juice in a blender. Add a small pinch of salt and a little pepper. Now turn the motor on and very slowly pour in the olive oil through the feeder tube. Don't be tempted to add the oil too quickly, or the mixture may curdle. Once it's all been added, you should have a smooth, dark cream coloured sauce. Pour into a bowl, add the crème fraîche and stir well to combine. Taste and adjust the seasoning if necessary; you are unlikely to need more salt.

Set the scallops aside at room temperature while you prepare the salad. Separate the radicchio leaves, wash gently and pat dry using a clean tea towel. Do the same with the rocket. Remove the fibrous outer layer from the fennel, slice in half lengthways, then cut into the finest long slices you can manage. Place the leaves and sliced fennel in a bowl, season with a little salt and pepper and add the lemon zest, lemon juice and extra virgin olive oil. Toss together lightly with your fingers, taste for seasoning and set aside while you cook the scallops.

Heat a large heavy-based frying pan (preferably non-stick) over a high heat. Season the scallops with salt and pepper and add the olive oil to the pan. When the pan is very hot (starting to smoke), add the scallops, in a single layer. Cook without moving for 1 minute, then turn and cook for approximately 40 seconds on the other side. The scallops should have a crunchy exterior and the flesh inside should be sweet and soft. Remove from the heat.

Divide the dressed salad leaves among individual plates, arrange 5 scallops on top of each portion and spoon over a little Gorgonzola dressing. Finish with a sprinkling of finely chopped parsley and toasted breadcrumbs. Serve at once – the scallops should be eaten as hot as possible.

Goat's cheese soufflé with lemon thyme

I love the simplicity of cooking and serving a soufflé on a soup plate. I first ate a soufflé prepared in this way in a small restaurant in Southwest France and was struck by its elegance. I like to serve it with a very simply dressed salad comprising only leaves. Sometimes there will be some good bread too, but it doesn't really need it.

Serves 6

40g unsalted butter, melted

210g Parmesan or pecorino, freshly grated

440g soft young lemony goat's cheese (without rind)

7 organic free-range eggs, separated

160ml double cream

small bunch of lemon thyme (or ordinary thyme), leaves only

1 tsp very finely chopped dried red chilli (optional)

sea salt and freshly ground black pepper

handful of warm toasted sourdough breadcrumbs, to finish (optional)

Preheat the oven to 200°C/Gas 6. Brush six ovenproof soup plates with the melted butter and sprinkle with half of the Parmesan.

Crumble the goat's cheese into a bowl, add the egg yolks and cream, and whisk until smooth. Add the lemon thyme, and dried chilli if using, then fold in the remaining Parmesan. Season with salt and pepper to taste.

Place the egg whites in a scrupulously clean bowl, add a pinch of salt and whisk to firm peaks. Fold a third of the whisked whites into the cheese mixture until evenly incorporated, then carefully fold in the rest of the whites in two batches until thoroughly combined.

Divide the soufflé mixture among the soup plates. Set on a large baking sheet and place on the middle shelf of your oven. Bake for 10–11 minutes until the soufflés are puffed and golden. Remove from the oven, taking care as the plates will be very hot. Serve immediately, scattered with toasted breadcrumbs for a contrast in texture if you like.

For sourdough breadcrumbs, whiz chunks of sourdough bread in a food processor to rough breadcrumbs. Tip into a bowl, season well and toss with a good splash of olive oil. Scatter on a baking tray and toast in the oven at 190°C/Gas 5 for about 15 minutes until golden and crunchy, shaking the tray frequently to ensure they toast evenly.

Robiola with malenca and pickled grapes

This is more a combination of very beautiful ingredients than a recipe. Robiola is a wonderfully luxurious triple milk cheese from Piedmont, Italy. It has a full, tangy flavour – slightly goaty, mushroomy, just a little citrusy and sweet all at the same time. Malenca is a cured meat from the adjacent region of Lombardy, similar to bresaola, which is a suitable substitute. I like to slice it slightly thicker than bresaola, as it stands up better to the rich flavour of the Robiola that way.

Serves 4

about 24 shelled hazelnuts (optional)

80ml mild-tasting extra virgin olive oil

1 tablespoon red wine vinegar

sea salt and freshly ground black pepper

3 celery sticks (from the sweet inner white heart)

handful or so of sweet young leaves, such as celery leaves, mâche or oak leaf

300g Robiola

12 slices of Malenca or bresaola

20 pickled grapes or pickled cherries (see page 29)

Preheat the oven to 200°C/Gas 6. If using hazelnuts, scatter on a baking sheet and toast for about 10 minutes until the skins begin to darken and split. While still warm, scrunch them in a clean cloth to rub off most of their skins.

Whisk the olive oil and wine vinegar together with a pinch each of salt and pepper to make a dressing. Taste and adjust the seasoning.

Slice the celery on the diagonal. Wash and dry the salad leaves, place in a bowl and add the celery. Toss lightly with the dressing.

Divide the salad among serving plates. Spoon the Robiola on top, arrange the cured meat attractively around the cheese and top with the pickled grapes. Scatter over the hazelnuts if using, and serve.

Manchego with quince paste

Quince, to me, is perhaps the most beautiful of all fruits. Heavy in size and pale green in colour, it hangs so gracefully from its tree. I tend to make this rough paste every year, firstly because it is delicious and secondly because ritual is one of nicest things about cooking with the seasons. I like to serve it with its classic partner manchego – preferably a slightly older cheese, as its sweet, chalky, crystally nature is just that much more intense.

Quince paste
12 quinces
1kg sugar

To serve
about 60g manchego
per serving
a drizzle of olive oil
(optional)

Wipe over the quinces with a clean damp cloth fruit to remove the downy covering, then roughly chop the fruit. Place in a large non-reactive saucepan, add the sugar, then pour in enough water to just cover the fruit. Place over a medium-low heat until the sugar has dissolved, then turn the heat up slightly and cook for 2^1/$_2$ hours or until the fruit is a beautiful burnt orange colour and has completely fallen apart.

Remove from the heat, allow to cool slightly, then spoon the quince paste into sterilised jars. Store in the fridge or a cool dark larder and use within 2 or 3 months. (You'll have enough here for plenty of cheese courses.)

To serve, slice the manchego and arrange on serving plates with a generous portion of quince paste. Everyone always tells me not to put olive oil on cheese, but I never listen – I think it's wonderful, so finish with a drizzle or two… if you approve.

Harder chalkier cheeses have a different savour when eaten thinly sliced, rather than in a thicker piece. It's nice to experience those differences, so try serving slices of varying thicknesses.

Honey

Over the past couple of years I have become increasingly drawn to using honey in cooking. Sugar is one-dimensional in flavour, unless of course you play with it, taking it to a deep rich caramel. By contrast, honey is complex and lends subtle flavour notes to dishes. Not only is it great to cook with, honey is also wonderful drizzled over cheeses, ice creams and perfectly ripe, seasonal fruit.

Honey is a natural product that very often sings of the terrain in which it was created. So, it is hardly surprising that there are almost as many varieties of honey as there are wines – each and every one with its very own distinctive flavour notes and character. Among my favourites are acacia, wildflower and our locally produced honeys, but the one I love best of all is chestnut honey. The colour of burnt caramel – with a flavour to match – it is sublime drizzled over slivers of aged pecorino or Parmesan.

Honey is produced all over the world – from Siberia to the tropics. In warmer climates this can happen throughout the year, but in the very coldest countries the season can be as short as 2 or 3 weeks.

The type of flower from which the bee has collected the nectar determines a honey variety's distinct aroma, flavour and colour. And the resulting characteristics of the honey closely resemble the flavours of the flowers, trees and herbs that the bees have visited. Most honeys are what are known as polyfloral honeys, which means that the bees have taken nectar from many different floral sources. However, the most prized of all honeys are those from bees that have predominantly fed from the nectar of one plant species. These are known as monofloral. Of these, as I have said, chestnut honey is my favourite. Its flavour is so very particular that it can be quite shocking the first time you taste it. Not really sweet at all, the taste resonates to me of molasses, with a mildly bitter finish.

◊

Equally passionate about honey, my friend and mentor Wendy Fogarty summed it up perfectly when she said, 'Honey tells us so much about the place it comes from. I love the fact that the complexity and majesty of nature can be so simply translated into this one single product.'

Like vinegar, I usually have several different varieties of honey in my storecupboard, which I love to dip in and out of. There is light acacia honey that I have on sticky rye toast in the morning with cold unsalted butter. Sitting alongside is a jar of my favourite chestnut honey. And I always have some of our local honey – from nearby Richmond Park where it is produced in small quantites. Another fairly local honey I have to hand is from Brockwell Park in Brixton, produced by one man – Orlando Clarke. Urban honeys are not to be sniffed at, for they can be quite delicious.

◊

I find I use honey in all manner of dishes in the kitchen. Another of my breakfast favourites is toasted sourdough topped with young creamy goat's cheese or ricotta and drizzled with honey.

A spoonful of honey stirred into warm porridge is delicious in the winter. During the warmer months, try soaking whole oats in freshly squeezed apple juice. Grate the flesh of an apple – skin and all – into the soaking oats and finish with a spoonful of honey. Cover and keep in the fridge overnight, then in the morning you will have a sweet, creamy breakfast cereal, known as Bircher muesli.

I also use honey in various dressings for salads and vegetables. At home, my daughter, Evie is the queen of salad dressings. She often makes one my mother taught her, consisting of a teaspoonful of honey, a little squeeze of orange juice and a drop or two of soy sauce. This sweet, slightly salty dressing clings to the leaves irresistibly. I recommend that you try it.

Occasionally I use honey to sweeten a creamy dressing. A little honey, a squeeze of lime and perhaps a little finely chopped red

chilli stirred into crème fraîche or yoghurt is delicious spooned over warm, roasted summer squash or pumpkin, for example.

In the autumn, I'll often reach for a jar of honey when I'm making a salad dressing, as salads in the cooler months usually benefit from a slightly more robust dressing. A little honey mixed with Dijon mustard, sherry vinegar and seasoning, and whisked with walnut oil makes for an interesting dressing, with all the right seasonal notes. Spoon it over a salad of tender roasted onion squash, young creamy walnuts and autumn salad leaves.

As for desserts, honey offers endless possibilities. Try adding a tablespoonful or so to a chocolate sorbet or a chocolate truffle cake to lend a warm, sweet flavour, for instance.

When roasting fruit, I often substitute honey for sugar. It is delicious drizzled over sliced quince with some pared lemon zest and fresh bay, as indeed it is over pears, plums, medlars or apricots.

And of course, if you are rounding off the meal with cheese and fruit, a drizzle of honey is often a perfect complement. There is no doubt that honey's complexity of flavour gives food a greater depth and often makes a dish taste more interesting.

Chicken with figs and honey

This dish, like so many, relies on using very good ingredients – lovely ripe figs and the best free-range organic chicken that you can afford. It is unquestionably simple, but delicious. A salad of leaves, dressed with nothing more than olive oil and lemon – and perhaps some good bread to mop up the juices – is all that is needed to accompany. *Illustrated on previous page*

Serves 6

1 organic free-range chicken, about 1.6kg, jointed into 6–8 pieces

sea salt and freshly ground black pepper

2 tbsp mild-tasting olive oil

1 medium yellow onion, peeled and sliced

few thyme sprigs

1 bay leaf

125ml white wine or verjuice

150ml good-quality chicken stock

2 tbsp white wine vinegar

1 tbsp mild-tasting honey, such as acacia

10 ripe figs

Preheat the oven to 180°C/Gas 4. Trim off the excess fat from the chicken, then season it generously all over with salt and pepper.

Heat the olive oil in a large frying pan over a medium heat, then brown the seasoned chicken pieces in batches, skin side down, for about 8 minutes, turning to colour them evenly all over. Remove the chicken to a flameproof casserole with a slotted spoon. Pour off most of the fat from the frying pan, then add the onion and cook over a low heat for 5 minutes to soften.

Add the onion to the casserole with the thyme and bay leaf. Pour over the wine or verjuice and the chicken stock. Place the casserole, uncovered, on the middle shelf of the oven and cook for about 30 minutes until the meat is tender but not quite falling from the bone. The skin should now be golden and the liquid reduced by about half.

Place the casserole over a low heat on the hob. Mix the wine vinegar and honey together and pour in. Tear each of the ripe figs into four and add to the casserole. Turn up the heat and bring to the boil. Allow to bubble until the liquor has reduced to a syrupy consistency – it should be glossy and taste both sweet and sour. Serve on warm plates, with a salad and some bread.

Honey in savoury dishes can be delicious, but it must be counterbalanced with a certain amount of acidity to redress the balance. The Italians call this balance of sweet and sour *agro-dolce*.

Baked Sauternes and honey custard

We first made this custard a couple of years ago, when Maggie Beer came to visit us at Petersham. A warm, vibrant bundle of energy, she is one of my favourite cooks – representing everything to me that's wonderful about cooking! This recipe is adapted from one in her lovely book, *Maggie's Orchard*. We serve this custard with roasted rhubarb during the late winter and early spring months.

Serves 6

350ml Sauternes

500ml double cream

1/2 vanilla pod, split lengthways

100g caster sugar

30ml honey (rhododendron, or any other monofloral honey with a pronounced flavour)

7 organic free-range egg yolks

Preheat the oven to 180°C/Gas 4. Pour the wine into a heavy-based saucepan and bring to the boil over a medium heat. Let bubble until reduced by half, then remove from the heat.

In a separate saucepan, slowly warm the cream with the vanilla pod, then stir into the reduced wine.

In a large bowl, beat the sugar and honey together to combine, then incorporate the egg yolks one at a time, beating well after each addition. Pour on the wine and cream mixture, stirring well with a whisk as you do so.

Pour the mixture into a shallow ovenproof dish, measuring about 25 x 15cm, and place in a roasting tray containing enough hot water to come halfway up the side of the dish. Place on the middle shelf of the oven and bake for about 45 minutes until the custard is set but still quite wobbly in the centre.

Allow to cool to room temperature before serving. The custard is also wonderfully refreshing served chilled on a hot day.

Baked pears with honey, marsala and bay

A beautiful, uncomplicated dessert for autumn or early winter. Serve it warm, not hot, with a generous spoonful of crème fraîche or good homemade vanilla ice cream (see page 34). Here I have used my favourite Martin Sec pears, but you could use Conference or Comice instead. I generally allow one pear per person, but you might like to bake a few extra and put them in the middle of the table for guests to help themselves to an extra half pear.

Serves 6–8

8 firm, ripe pears

600ml marsala

220ml fragrant honey, such as rhododendron or a mountain or forest honey

1 cinnamon stick

1 vanilla pod, split lengthways

finely pared zest of 1 lemon

sprig of bay leaves (about 4 or 5 leaves)

Preheat the oven to 200°C/Gas 6. Place the pears in a roasting dish in which they fit quite snugly, with their stalks uppermost. Pour over the marsala and drizzle over the honey, then add the cinnamon stick, vanilla pod, lemon zest and bay leaves. Cover the dish tightly with foil.

Place the roasting dish on the middle shelf of the oven and roast for 20 minutes. Remove the foil and bake, uncovered, for a further 20 minutes. The pears should be soft and the skin slightly wrinkly. Allow to cool to room temperature.

Serve the pears on individual plates with the marsala and honey syrup spooned over.

Chocolate

There is an aura of luxury about chocolate – it feels indulgent, almost clandestine. We make a decision to eat chocolate in a way that we don't make about eating other food ... a considered 'Shall I?' and if the answer is 'Yes', we are likely to feel slightly decadent about our decision. Each little mouthful is savoured, sometimes with an association of guilt. Yet above all, chocolate is treasured – a gift for loved ones on special occasions. Somehow it gives a message to the recipient that they are valued and special – and therefore so is chocolate itself.

When it comes to cooking, I recommend that you buy the finest quality chocolate you can afford – dark purple-black in colour, glossy and bitter, with an almost smoky quality. In my view, chocolate desserts should be intensely rich, but not too sweet – and eaten in small quantities for ultimate pleasure.

For centuries chocolate has been prized around the world. It is produced, of course, from the beans of the cocoa tree (*Theobroma cacao*) native to South America, *Theobroma* meaning 'food of the gods'. As long as 3,500 years ago chocolate was produced in Mexico, though right up until the 1800s it was only ever consumed in the form of a drink; in fact the word chocolate means 'hot beverage'.

Chocolate as we know it today is made from the seeds (or beans) of the cacao pods. The beans are fermented, dried, roasted and hulled in order to separate the nibs from their shells. The nibs are then ground and melted to make a paste known as chocolate liquor. On cooling, this sets and hardens to become unsweetened cooking chocolate. At this stage it consists of nothing more than half cocoa butter and half cocoa solids. Other things are later mixed in, such as sugar, vanilla and milk; in lesser quality products emulsifiers and stabilisers are often added, too.

The chocolate is now 'conched' (or kneaded) for at least 12 hours (as long as 3 days for fine quality chocolate) to make it as smooth as possible and eliminate any gritty texture. Finally it is 'tempered' or cooled and reheated in several controlled stages so that it hardens to a shiny gloss and snaps when broken. The chocolate is then aged for 60–90 days.

You may have heard of couverture in connection with chocolate for cooking. This is chocolate with a high cocoa butter content, designed to provide a thin even coating and a high finished gloss. It is also good for more general use, due to its superior quality.

◊

Rich and intensely flavoured, good-quality chocolate should be eaten in small pieces. Don't rush it – let it linger in your mouth and savour its lovely bitter, smoky aroma and flavour. Like many good things, a little goes a long way…

At the restaurant, we use the best quality chocolate that we can find, usually Valrhona, an intense and beautiful chocolate from France (64 per cent cocoa solids minimum), or Amedei an Italian chocolate made by a family in Tuscany.

Dark chocolate has a shelf life of about a year. It is best kept in a cool larder or drawer – in one large block rather than pieces and wrapped in foil. Storing chocolate at a higher temperature can cause cocoa butter to rise to the surface causing dull brown patches known as a 'bloom' to appear, making the chocolate unusable. Conversely, if you keep chocolate in the fridge the humidity can cause white 'sugar bloom' spots to form on the surface.

◊

Melting chocolate The best way to melt chocolate is in a double boiler, or heatproof bowl set over a pan of gently simmering water. It is important that the bowl in which the chocolate is to melt does not sit directly in the water. Break up or chop the chocolate first to encourage it to melt evenly and don't stir it during melting as this can dull the shine. If you are melting chocolate with cream, then you can stir the pieces of chocolate directly into the hot cream, otherwise add chocolate to cool rather than hot liquids and melt slowly and gently in a pan over direct heat.

◊

When it comes to pairing chocolate with other flavours, dark, salty caramels, almonds, hazelnuts, coffee and candied citrus fruit work best. With the exception of citrus fruits and a few others, I find fresh fruits less compatible with chocolate. Slightly bitter oranges complement dark chocolate beautifully; cherries and chocolate are also natural partners. And if a chocolate dessert calls for some cream on the side, I'll invariably serve it with a bowl of thick unpasteurised cream as opposed to crème fraîche, whose slightly sharp acidity tends to rub against the smooth flavour of the chocolate rather than enhance it.

Hazelnuts go particularly well with chocolate, providing a texture and flavour that are truly compatible. Their earthy flavour serves to balance the rich bitterness of good-quality dark chocolate.

Chocolate mousse

Perfecting a chocolate mousse seemed to take us forever. I was looking for a mousse that was rich, yet very definitely light, with a certain density about it. Also, I wanted to serve it freeform on a plate, but to do that the flavour had to be elegant ... even smoky. This is what we finally came up with, thanks largely to the work of Sophie Cookes who was with us in the kitchen at the time. It needs to be served with something to counterbalance its intensity. Here I've chosen my favourite accompaniment – salty, almost burnt, caramel ... and cream, of course.

Serves 8

330g good-quality dark chocolate (minimum 64% cocoa solids), in pieces

8 organic free-range eggs, separated

100g caster sugar

pinch of sea salt

Salty caramel

250g caster sugar

375ml water

generous pinch of sea salt

Take this salty caramel as far as you dare. It calls for a little courage but I take it to where I can just smell the burn. Visually, I love a rich, dark caramel; one that is too pale looks – and tastes – insipid. This is a good example of all our senses playing a role in our cooking – sight, sound, smell and, of course, taste.

Melt the chocolate slowly in a heatproof bowl set over a pan of gently simmering water (see page 236), then remove from the heat and leave to cool slightly. Meanwhile, beat the egg yolks and half the sugar together in a bowl until pale and thick. Slowly incorporate the melted chocolate.

In a clean bowl, whisk the egg whites with the salt until soft peaks form, then gradually whisk in the remaining sugar. Carefully fold the egg whites into the chocolate mixture, a third at a time, until evenly combined. Pour into a large bowl, cover and place in the fridge to set.

For the salty caramel, place the sugar and 125ml water in a small heavy-based pan over a very low heat and, without stirring, allow the sugar to dissolve. Once dissolved, turn up the heat to fairly high and bring to the boil. Cook until the caramel begins to colour; this will take at least 5 minutes. When it starts to brown around the sides, watch it carefully – as it will then darken quite quickly.

Once the caramel has reached a deep mahogany colour, quickly and carefully pour in the remaining 250ml water. Cook, stirring, for another 2 minutes to loosen the caramel and ensure that it doesn't set hard. Finally throw in the salt, stir once or twice, then take off the heat. Pour into a heatproof bowl and allow to cool, then chill.

To serve, spoon the chocolate mousse onto plates and serve with the salty caramel and cream.

Rich chocolate ice cream

I love ice cream – primarily because I really enjoy making it, which we do almost everyday of the year at the restaurant. More often than not, our ices are fruit based but occasionally we make this chocolate ice cream. It took quite a few attempts to get it right because I wanted something very rich and luxurious, yet a custard base will only take so much chocolate before it refuses to freeze.

Serves 4–6

150ml whole milk

350ml double cream

1 vanilla pod, split lengthways

60g good-quality dark chocolate (minimum 64% cocoa solids)

6 organic free-range egg yolks

120g caster sugar

2 tbsp unsweetened cocoa powder

Pour the milk and cream into a heavy-based saucepan, add the vanilla pod, place over a medium heat and bring to the boil. Chop the chocolate into rough chunks, add to the hot creamy milk and stir once or twice to encourage it to melt.

While the chocolate is melting, beat the egg yolks and sugar together in a bowl for a minute or so until thick and pale. Sift the cocoa powder over the surface and stir to combine. Pour on the hot cream, whisking as you do so, then pour back into the pan.

Turn the heat to very low and stir, using a figure-of-eight motion, until the custard thickens. You'll need to be patient as this will take 8–10 minutes. Don't be tempted to rush the process by turning up the heat as it may cause the custard to curdle. As soon as the custard is thick enough to lightly coat the back of a wooden spoon, remove from the heat and strain through a fine sieve into a bowl.

Allow to cool completely, then pour the custard into your ice-cream maker and churn until thickened. When it is ready, freeze in a suitable container. The ice cream will be ready to eat in a couple of hours and will keep well for a day or so, but no longer. Homemade ice cream is better eaten relatively soon after it has been made. Spoon into chilled bowls to serve.

Zuppa inglese

In many ways this Italian version of an English trifle is a departure from the desserts we usually make in the restaurant. The inspiration for it comes from a recipe written by Mario Batalli, who is a fine chef and food writer. Rich, creamy and indulgent, with just enough orange syrup and lemon zest added to make it light – it has a cheekiness about it that I find endearing. *Illustrated on previous page*

Serves 8

600ml whole milk

grated zest of 2 oranges

grated zest of 1 lemon

1 vanilla pod, split in half lengthways

8 organic free-range eggs

125g caster sugar

120g plain flour

5 tbsp good-quality unsweetened cocoa powder

80g good-quality dark chocolate (minimum 64% cocoa solids), chopped

80ml limoncello

20 savoiardi (sponge finger biscuits)

Candied oranges

2 oranges

250g caster sugar

250ml water

First prepare the candied oranges. Slice into fine rounds and blanch in a pan of boiling water for 1 minute or so. Drain and refresh in cold water. Repeat this blanching process twice more. Dissolve the sugar in the water in a small heavy-based pan over a medium heat, then bring to the boil. Add the oranges, turn down the heat slightly and cook for 10–15 minutes or until the syrup is viscous and the oranges are translucent. Take off the heat and set aside to cool.

Pour the milk into a heavy-based pan and add the orange and lemon zest. Scrape the seeds from the vanilla pod and add to the pan, with the empty pod. Heat to a simmer, then immediately remove from the heat and set aside to infuse for 15 minutes.

Put the eggs, sugar and flour into a large bowl and whisk, using an electric beater, until the mixture is pale and thick. Slowly pour on the milk, whisking as you do so. Pour back into the pan and whisk over a low heat until the custard thickens enough to coat the back of a wooden spoon and no longer taste floury. Immediately pour into two bowls, dividing it equally and discarding the vanilla pod. Add the cocoa powder and chocolate to one bowl and stir until the cocoa is evenly distributed and the chocolate has melted. Set the bowls of vanilla and chocolate custard aside to cool.

Drain the oranges, reserving the syrup, and chop into small pieces. Stir the limoncello into the syrup. Take a tablespoonful of the syrup and stir it into the vanilla custard. Split the savoiardi in half lengthways and sprinkle with the remaining orange syrup.

Arrange a layer of the soaked savoiardi over the bottom of a pretty serving bowl. Top with a layer of vanilla custard, then a scattering of chopped orange. Add another layer of savoiardi, followed by chocolate custard, then orange. Continue in this way until you've used all the ingredients, finishing with a few spoonfuls each of the vanilla and chocolate custards. Swirl together to create a marbled effect, then refrigerate for at least an hour before serving.

Warm chocolate puddings

These comforting little treats literally ooze chocolate from their centre. Gooey and molten, they are wonderful served simply with cream. I also like them with coffee ice cream, or cream flavoured with a touch of honey.

Serves 6

150g unsalted butter, plus extra to grease

300g good-quality dark chocolate (minimum 64% cocoa solids)

4 organic free-range eggs

3 organic free-range egg yolks

150g caster sugar

50g plain flour

Lightly butter 6 individual pudding moulds, 200ml capacity. Using a sharp knife, chop the chocolate into 2cm chunks. Melt the chocolate and butter together in a heatproof bowl set over a pan of gently simmering water (see page 236), then remove from the heat and leave to cool slightly.

Meanwhile, using an electric mixer, beat together the whole eggs, egg yolks and sugar until pale and mousse-like. This will take about 5 minutes – the beaters should leave a ribbon-like trail on the surface of the mixture as you lift them.

Now gently and carefully pour in the chocolate, folding it in lightly but thoroughly to combine. Sift the flour from a good height over the surface and fold in carefully. Spoon the mixture into the prepared moulds and place in the fridge for an hour.

Preheat the oven to 200°C/Gas 6. Stand the moulds on a baking tray and bake in the oven for 18 minutes until the puddings are puffed up with a slight crust. Turn out onto warm plates and serve immediately... they will smell and taste delicious!

Less is more with food, especially desserts like this. To my mind, your last mouthful should leave you wanting perhaps just one more spoonful. Food should linger as a lovely memory – a thought, a dream.

Chocolate panna cotta with warm berries and honey

Rich, creamy and a little wobbly, this dessert needs to be served cool from the fridge – ideally within 24 hours, as the gelatine continues to set the mixture as long as it sits in the fridge. Blackberries in warm honey go beautifully, but you can serve it just as it is if you prefer, or with salty caramel (see page 239). Ripe sweet strawberries and cream would be the perfect accompaniment in summer.

Serves 4

a little oil, to oil the moulds

200g good-quality dark chocolate (minimum 64% cocoa solids)

2 sheets of leaf gelatine

190ml whole milk

250ml double cream

100g caster sugar

1 vanilla pod, split lengthways

Blackberries and honey

180ml honey (I like to use chestnut honey, or lighter acacia honey)

200g blackberries

Lightly oil 4 individual panna cotta moulds or other individual pudding basins, 200ml capacity.

Chop the chocolate into small pieces and melt slowly, without stirring, in a heatproof bowl set over a pan of gently simmering water (see page 236). Remove the bowl of melted chocolate from the heat and set aside to cool slightly. Soak the gelatine leaves in cold water to cover for about 5 minutes to soften.

In the meantime, put the milk, cream and sugar into a heavy-based pan. Scrape the seeds from the vanilla pod and add these to the pan with the empty pod. Place over a medium heat and bring to a gentle simmer, stirring once or twice to help dissolve the sugar. Remove from the heat and strain through a fine sieve onto the melted chocolate, stirring well to combine.

If necessary, return the chocolate mixture to the pan and reheat gently – it needs to be very hot but not quite boiling. Take off the heat. Squeeze the gelatine to remove excess water and add to the hot cream, stirring to dissolve.

Strain the mixture through a fine sieve into a jug, then pour into the prepared moulds. Allow to cool completely, then refrigerate for at least 2 hours before serving.

For the accompanying berries, warm the honey in a small saucepan. Add two-thirds of the blackberries and cook gently until they have begun to bleed into the warm honey. Remove from the heat and stir through the remaining blackberries.

To serve, quickly dip the base of each mould into hot water to loosen the base and sides, then run a small sharp knife around the top and invert the panna cotta onto a plate. Spoon the warm blackberries and honey over the panna cottas and serve, with a bowl of rich yellow cream on the side.

Chocolate and hazelnut cake

I like to take this cake from the oven when it is still very definitely wobbly in the centre. It oozes a little when you cut into it – the soft, fluid dense chocolate in the middle is my favourite bit, eaten with a spoonful of rich, thick buttercup yellow cream. It is delicious warm or cold. You can even keep it in the fridge for a couple of days – the texture will be firmer in the centre, but it still tastes good.

Serves 8–10

375g unsalted butter, plus extra to grease

75g plain flour, plus extra to dust

60g shelled hazelnuts

375g good-quality dark chocolate (minimum 64% cocoa solids)

9 organic free-range eggs, separated

300g caster sugar

pinch of sea salt

icing sugar, to dust

Preheat the oven to 170°C/Gas 3. Butter and flour a 26cm round cake tin. Spread the hazelnuts out on a baking tray and put them in the warm oven for 3–4 minutes, just to tickle out their flavour. Let cool slightly, then rub in a cloth to remove the skins. Grind the nuts, using a pestle and mortar or blender, leaving the texture slightly uneven – this makes for a more interesting cake.

Chop both the chocolate and the butter into small chunks and place in a heatproof bowl set over a pan of gently simmering water to melt (see page 236). Don't stir until the very end, just let them melt together slowly. Once melted, stir once or twice to combine and remove from the heat. Allow to cool slightly.

Meanwhile, beat the egg yolks and sugar together in a bowl until pale and thick. Pour in the melted chocolate and stir gently to combine. Sift the flour over the surface and add the ground nuts. Fold in lightly until evenly combined.

Place the egg whites in a very clean bowl with the salt. Whisk, slowly to begin with until the whites have broken down, then more quickly until soft peaks form. Carefully fold into the chocolate mixture and pour into the prepared cake tin.

Bake on the middle shelf of the oven for 40–50 minutes or until just set, but still wobbly in the centre. Leave in the tin for 10 minutes, then turn out and place on a wire rack to cool. Serve warm or cold, dusted with icing sugar.

Index

agresto, 147

agretti: asparagus with poached
skate and, 20–1
lobster salad with fennel and
blood oranges, 50

aïoli, 168
tomato aïoli, 56–7, 81

almonds, 143
clementines with Medjool dates,
pomegranates and honeyed
almonds, 97
romesco, 148
warm date and almond
puddings, 152

anchovies, 42
borlotti with garlic, sage and
olive oil, 109
mint and anchovy dressing, 92

apples, 194–205
apple, fennel, speck and hazelnut
salad, 197
apple galette, 204
apple ice cream with toasted
cobnuts and caramel sauce, 202
kohlrabi, apple and crab salad,
198
little baked apples, 201
tomato and apple ketchup, 138

artichokes: deep-fried artichokes
and lemon with mint and
anchovy dressing, 92

artichokes, Jerusalem see
Jerusalem artichokes

asparagus, 10–25
asparagus, rice and pancetta
soup, 16
gratin of white asparagus, 22–3
grilled rump of lamb with
asparagus, 25
with agretti, pounded chilli oil
and poached skate, 20–1
with ginger and garlic, 19
with Tabasco butter, 13
with tomato dressing and crème
fraîche, 14

avocados: pink grapefruit, avocado
and watercress salad, 74

balsamic vinegar, 160
balsamic mayonnaise, 182
bruschetta with aged balsamic
vinegar, 161

basil oil, 129

beans, 106–8
borlotti, clams and fino, 113
borlotti with garlic, sage and
olive oil, 109
lobster with white beans,
tarragon and tomatoes, 132
pigeon with borlotti and cavolo,
190
ribollita, 66
wild garlic and white bean curry,
114

beef: carpaccio of beef with red
pepper relish, 65
skirt steak with hazelnut
picada and wilted escarole,
151
stracotto, 176

beetroot: roasted vegetable salad
with rocket and tomatoes, 76
salad of roasted beetroot,
walnuts, watercress and
mascarpone, 144

blackberries: chocolate panna
cotta with warm berries and
honey, 246

blood oranges with warm honey
and rosemary, 98

borlotti beans, 108
borlotti, clams and fino, 113
borlotti with garlic, sage and
olive oil, 109
pigeon with borlotti and cavolo,
190

brandied cherries, 37

bread: bruschetta with aged
balsamic vinegar, 161
bruschetta of sheep's milk
ricotta, lemon oil and
bresaola, 209
roasted grouse with Barolo on
toast, 192

salad of warm torn bread,
poached egg and Parmesan
dressing, 216
sourdough breadcrumbs, 219
tomato and bread soup, 127

bresaola, bruschetta of sheep's
milk ricotta, lemon oil and,
209

broccoli: slow-roasted pork belly
with sprouting broccoli and
puréed garlic, 175

bruschetta see bread

Brussels sprouts: aged pecorino
with raw sprouts, celery and
speck, 210

butter, 62
Tabasco butter, 13

cake, chocolate and hazelnut, 248

candied oranges, 244

candlenuts, 143

cannellini beans: lobster with
white beans, tarragon and
tomatoes, 132
ribollita, 66

caramel: apple ice cream with
toasted cobnuts and caramel
sauce, 202
salty caramel, 239

carpaccio of beef with red pepper
relish, 65

carpaccio of smoked haddock with
chilli and winter purslane, 52

cashews, 143

cavolo nero: pigeon with borlotti
and cavolo, 190
ribollita, 66

cedro, chocolate-dipped candied,
104

chard: chick pea and chard soup,
110
lamb with tomatoes, chard and
horseradish dressing, 136

cheese, 206–23
aged pecorino with raw sprouts,
celery and speck, 210
bruschetta of sheep's milk
ricotta, lemon oil and
bresaola, 209

goat's cheese soufflé with lemon thyme, 219

grilled partridge with chilli, marjoram and ricotta, 184

manchego with quince paste, 222

nectarine and tomato salad with Parma ham and buffalo mozzarella, 129

pickled pumpkin with burrata, 162

roasted Jerusalem artichokes with goat's cheese, roasted tomatoes and agresto, 147

Robiola with Malenca and pickled grapes, 220

salad of roasted beetroot, walnuts, watercress and mascarpone, 144

salad of warm torn bread, poached egg and Parmesan dressing, 216

scallops with rocket, fennel, toasted breadcrumbs and Gorgonzola dressing, 218

wafer-thin slices of porcini with aged Parmesan and crème fraîche, 215

cherries, 26–39

brandied cherries, 37

cherry cordial, 39

cherry granita, 36

clafoutis, 33

pickled cherries, 29

vanilla ice cream with poached cherries and chocolate sauce, 34

warm pheasant salad with tardivo, pickled cherries and toasted hazelnuts, 30

chick pea and chard soup, 110

chick pea flour: farinata, 119

chicken: chicken with figs and honey, 230

chicken with garlic and fennel, 172

see also poussins

chillies: asparagus with agretti, pounded chilli oil and poached skate, 20–1

carpaccio of smoked haddock with chilli and winter purslane, 52

crab cakes with corn purée and chilli oil, 48

fried egg with sage, chilli and garlicky yoghurt, 170

grilled partridge with chilli, marjoram and ricotta, 184

Poole prawns with chilli, salt and lemon, 44

slow-cooked shoulder of lamb with red wine vinegar, 165

wild garlic and white bean curry, 114

chocolate, 234–49

chocolate and hazelnut cake, 248

chocolate-dipped candied cedro and clementines, 104

chocolate mousse, 239

chocolate panna cotta with warm berries and honey, 246

rich chocolate ice cream, 240

vanilla ice cream with poached cherries and chocolate sauce, 34

warm chocolate puddings, 245

zuppa inglese, 244

citrus fruit, 86–105

clafoutis, 33

clams, 40, 42

borlotti, clams and fino, 113

clementines: chocolate-dipped candied clementines, 104

with Medjool dates, pomegranates and honeyed almonds, 97

cobnuts, 140

apple ice cream with toasted cobnuts and caramel sauce, 202

coco beans: wild garlic and white bean curry, 114

coconut milk: monkfish curry with coconut, lime and curry leaves, 59

squash and tomato curry with lime and coconut, 130

wild garlic and white bean curry, 114

cordial, cherry, 39

corn cobs: crab cakes with corn purée and chilli oil, 48

crab, 40, 42

crab cakes with corn purée and chilli oil, 48

kohlrabi, apple and crab salad, 198

cream: baked Sauternes and honey custard, 231

chocolate panna cotta, 246

cucumber: Middle Eastern salad of lettuce, herbs and, 73

rabbit with saffron, tomatoes, basil and, 134

curries: monkfish curry with coconut, lime and curry leaves, 59

squash and tomato curry with lime and coconut, 130

wild garlic and white bean curry, 114

custard, baked Sauternes and honey, 231

dates: clementines with Medjool dates, pomegranates and honeyed almonds, 97

warm date and almond puddings, 152

dried fruit: little baked apples, 201

drinks: cherry cordial, 39

lemonade, 89

duck: mallard with porcini and red wine, 188

eggs: fried egg with sage, chilli and garlicky yoghurt, 170

salad of warm torn bread, poached egg and Parmesan dressing, 216

escarole: skirt steak with hazelnut picada and wilted escarole, 151

farinata, 119
farro, 108
  ribollita, 66
fennel: apple, fennel, speck and
    hazelnut salad, 197
  borlotti, clams and fino, 113
  chicken with garlic and fennel,
    172
  lobster salad with blood oranges
    and, 50
  roasted vegetable salad with
    rocket and tomatoes, 76
  scallops with rocket, fennel and
    toasted breadcrumbs, 218
figs, chicken with honey and,
  230
fish and shellfish, 40–59
flowers, salad of summer leaves
    and, 78

game, 178–93
garlic, 166–77
  aïoli, 168
  asparagus with ginger and garlic,
    19
  baked garlic and shallots with
    fino, 169
  borlotti with garlic, sage and
    olive oil, 109
  chicken with garlic and fennel,
    172
  fried egg with sage, chilli and
    garlicky yoghurt, 170
  grilled poussins with lemon,
    marjoram, flat bread and
    garlicky yoghurt, 95
  pigeon with borlotti and cavolo,
    190
  slow-roasted pork belly with
    sprouting broccoli and puréed
    garlic, 175
  stracotto, 176
  wild sea bass with salmoriglio,
    68
  see also wild garlic
ginger, asparagus with garlic and,
  19
girolles, roasted quail with spinach
    and, 189

goat's cheese: goat's cheese
    soufflé with lemon thyme, 219
  roasted Jerusalem artichokes
    with goat's cheese, 147
grains and pulses, 106–19
granita, cherry, 36
grapefruit: pink grapefruit,
    avocado and watercress salad,
    74
  pink grapefruit and sherry
    sherbet, 100
grapes: pickled grapes, 29
  Robiola with Malenca and
    pickled grapes, 220
gratin of white asparagus, 22–3
grouse, 181
  roasted grouse with Barolo on
    toast, 192
guinea fowl, 181
  guinea fowl supremes with
    braised tardivo and balsamic
    mayonnaise, 182

haddock see smoked haddock
halibut, 42
  roasted halibut with preserved
    lemon and crème fraîche
    sauce, 54
ham see Parma ham
hazelnuts, 140, 143, 237
  apple, fennel, speck and hazelnut
    salad, 197
  chocolate and hazelnut cake,
    248
  hazelnut tart, 154–5
  Robiola with Malenca and
    pickled grapes, 220
  romesco, 148
  skirt steak with hazelnut picada
    and wilted escarole, 151
  warm pheasant salad with
    tardivo, pickled cherries and
    toasted hazelnuts, 30
herring, 42
honey, 224–33
  baked pears with honey, marsala
    and bay, 232
  baked Sauternes and honey
    custard, 231

blood oranges with warm honey
    and rosemary, 98
  chicken with figs and honey, 230
  chocolate panna cotta with
    warm berries and honey, 246
  clementines with Medjool dates,
    pomegranates and honeyed
    almonds, 97
horseradish: lamb with tomatoes,
    chard and horseradish
    dressing, 136
  pan-fried mackerel with red
    wine vinegar, horseradish and
    crème fraîche, 164

ice cream: apple ice cream with
    toasted cobnuts and caramel
    sauce, 202
  pecan and maple syrup ice
    cream, 156
  rich chocolate ice cream, 240
  vanilla ice cream with poached
    cherries and chocolate sauce,
    34

Jerusalem artichokes with goat's
    cheese, roasted tomatoes and
    agresto, 147

ketchup, tomato and apple, 138
kohlrabi, apple and crab salad, 198

lamb: grilled rump of lamb with
    asparagus, 25
  lamb with tomatoes, chard and
    horseradish dressing, 136
  slow-cooked shoulder of lamb
    with red wine vinegar, 165
langoustines with spinach, purple
    basil and tomato aïoli, 81
leaves, 71–83
lemon: deep-fried artichokes and
    lemon with mint and anchovy
    dressing, 92
  grilled poussins with lemon,
    marjoram, flat bread and
    garlicky yoghurt, 95
  lemon and orange curd, 90
  lemon-infused olive oil, 63

lemonade, 89
roasted halibut with preserved lemon and crème fraîche sauce, 54
lentils: grilled rabbit with lentils cooked in red wine, 118
lettuce, Middle Eastern salad of cucumber, herbs and, 73
limes: monkfish curry with coconut, lime and curry leaves, 59
squash and tomato curry with lime and coconut, 130
lobster, 42
lobster salad with fennel and blood oranges, 50
lobster with white beans, tarragon and tomatoes, 132
lovage, salsa verde of, 25

mackerel, 42
pan-fried mackerel with red wine vinegar, horseradish and crème fraîche, 164
mallard with porcini and red wine, 188
manchego with quince paste, 222
maple syrup: pecan and maple syrup ice cream, 156
marsala, baked pears with honey, bay and, 232
mayonnaise: aïoli, 168
balsamic mayonnaise, 182
crab cakes with corn purée and chilli oil, 48
Middle Eastern salad of cucumber, lettuce and herbs, 73
mint and anchovy dressing, 92
monkfish, 43
monkfish curry with coconut, lime and curry leaves, 59
mousse, chocolate, 239
mushrooms: mallard with porcini and red wine, 188
porcini, 214
roasted grouse with Barolo on toast, 192
roasted quail with girolles and spinach, 189

warm slices of porcini with aged Parmesan and crème fraîche, 215
mussels, 40, 42

nectarine and tomato salad with Parma ham and buffalo mozzarella, 129
nuts, 140–57
see also hazelnuts, walnuts etc.

oils: basil, 129
chilli, 20–1, 48
see also olive oil
olive oil, 60–9
borlotti with garlic, sage and olive oil, 109
carpaccio of beef with red pepper relish, 65
lemon-infused olive oil, 63
ribollita, 66
wild sea bass with salmoriglio, 68
onions: sea bass with mint, tomatoes and red onions, 133
stracotto, 176
oranges: blood oranges with warm honey and rosemary, 98
candied oranges, 244
lemon and orange curd, 90
lobster salad with fennel and blood oranges, 50

pancetta: asparagus, rice and pancetta soup, 16
grilled partridge with chilli, marjoram and ricotta, 184
panna cotta, chocolate, 246
Parma ham: nectarine and tomato salad with, 129
pink grapefruit, avocado and watercress salad, 74
salad of warm torn bread, poached egg and Parmesan dressing, 216
partridge with chilli, marjoram and ricotta, 184
pasta, tomato sauce for, 123
peanuts, 143

pears with honey, marsala and bay, 232
pecans, 143
pecan and maple syrup ice cream, 156
peppers: carpaccio of beef with red pepper relish, 65
squid with peppers, red wine and wild marjoram, 58
pheasant salad with tardivo, pickled cherries and toasted hazelnuts, 30
picada, hazelnut, 151
pickled cherries, 29
pickled grapes, 29
pickled pumpkin with burrata, 162
pigeon with borlotti and cavolo, 190
pine nuts, 143
pink grapefruit and sherry sherbet, 100
pink grapefruit, avocado and watercress salad, 74
pomegranates, clementines with Medjool dates and, 97
Poole prawns with chilli, salt and lemon, 44
porcini, 214
mallard with porcini and red wine, 188
warm slices of porcini with aged Parmesan and crème fraîche, 215
pork: slow-roasted pork belly with sprouting broccoli and puréed garlic, 175
potatoes, salt-baked wild salmon with roasted tomato aïoli, purslane and, 56–7
poussins with lemon, marjoram, flat bread and garlicky yoghurt, 95
prawns, 42
Poole prawns with chilli, salt and lemon, 44
pulses and grains, 106–19
pumpkin: pickled pumpkin with burrata, 162

purslane: carpaccio of smoked
   haddock with chilli and winter
   purslane, 52
   salt-baked wild salmon with
   roasted tomato aïoli, potatoes
   and purslane, 56–7

quail, 181
   roasted quail with girolles and
   spinach, 189
quince paste, manchego with, 222

rabbit: grilled rabbit with lentils
   cooked in red wine, 118
   rabbit with saffron, cucumber,
   tomatoes and basil, 134
relish, red pepper, 65
ribollita, 66
rice: asparagus, rice and pancetta
   soup, 16
   salad of poached salmon, black
   rice and watercress, 82
ricotta: bruschetta of sheep's milk
   ricotta, lemon oil and
   bresaola, 209
   grilled partridge with chilli,
   marjoram and ricotta, 184
Robiola with Malenca and pickled
   grapes, 220
rocket: roasted vegetable salad
   with rocket and tomatoes, 76
   scallops with rocket, fennel,
   toasted breadcrumbs and
   Gorgonzola dressing, 218
   squid with rocket and romesco,
   148
romesco, squid with rocket and,
   148

salads, 71–83
   apple, fennel, speck and hazelnut
   salad, 197
   kohlrabi, apple and crab salad,
   198
   lobster salad with fennel and
   blood oranges, 50
   Middle Eastern salad of
   cucumber, lettuce and herbs,
   73

nectarine and tomato salad with
   Parma ham and buffalo
   mozzarella, 129
pickled pumpkin with burrata, 162
pink grapefruit, avocado and
   watercress salad, 74
poached salmon, black rice and
   watercress, 82
roasted beetroot, walnuts,
   watercress and mascarpone,
   144
roasted vegetable salad with
   rocket and tomatoes, 76
squid with rocket and romesco,
   148
summer leaves and flowers, 78
warm pheasant salad with
   tardivo, pickled cherries and
   toasted hazelnuts, 30
warm torn bread, poached egg
   and Parmesan dressing, 216
salmon, 42
   salad of poached salmon, black
   rice and watercress, 82
   salt-baked wild salmon with
   roasted tomato aïoli, potatoes
   and purslane, 56–7
salmoriglio, wild sea bass with, 68
salsa verde, lovage, 25
salt-baked wild salmon, 56–7
salty caramel, 239
sardines, 42
sauces: baked Sauternes and
   honey custard, 231
   caramel, 202
   chocolate, 34
   romesco, 148
   sauce vierge, 124
   tomato and apple ketchup, 138
   tomato sauce for pasta, 123
scallops, 40, 42
   scallops with rocket, fennel,
   toasted breadcrumbs and
   Gorgonzola dressing, 218
sea bass: sea bass with mint,
   tomatoes and red onions, 133
   wild sea bass with salmoriglio,
   68
shallots: baked garlic and shallots

with fino, 169
shellfish and fish, 40–59
sherbet, pink grapefruit and
   sherry, 100
sherry: baked garlic and shallots
   with fino, 169
   borlotti, clams and fino, 113
   pink grapefruit and sherry
   sherbet, 100
skate: asparagus with agretti,
   pounded chilli oil and poached
   skate, 20–1
skirt steak with hazelnut picada
   and wilted escarole, 151
smoked haddock, carpaccio of, 52
soufflé, goat's cheese with lemon
   thyme, 219
soups: asparagus, rice and
   pancetta soup, 16
   borlotti, clams and fino, 113
   chick pea and chard soup, 110
   ribollita, 66
   tomato and bread soup, 127
sourdough breadcrumbs, 219
speck: aged pecorino with raw
   sprouts, celery and speck, 210
   apple, fennel, speck and hazelnut
   salad, 197
spinach: langoustines with cooked
   spinach, purple basil and
   tomato aïoli, 81
   roasted quail with girolles and
   spinach, 189
squash and tomato curry with
   lime and coconut, 130
squid: squid with peppers, red
   wine and wild marjoram, 58
   squid with rocket and romesco,
   148
stracotto, 176
sweet potatoes: roasted vegetable
   salad with rocket and
   tomatoes, 76
Swiss chard see chard

Tabasco butter, asparagus with, 13
tardivo: guinea fowl supremes
   with braised tardivo, 182
   warm pheasant salad with

warm pheasant salad with
  tardivo, 30
tarts: apple galette, 204
  hazelnut tart, 154–5
toast, roasted grouse with Barolo
  on, 192
tomatoes, 120–39
  asparagus with tomato dressing
    and crème fraîche, 14
  borlotti, clams and fino, 113
  chick pea and chard soup, 110
  chicken with garlic and fennel,
    172
  lamb with tomatoes, chard and
    horseradish dressing, 136
  langoustines with cooked
    spinach, purple basil and
    tomato aïoli, 81
  lobster with white beans,
    tarragon and tomatoes, 132
  monkfish curry with coconut,
    lime and curry leaves, 59
  nectarine and tomato salad with
    Parma ham and buffalo
    mozzarella, 129
  rabbit with saffron, cucumber,
    tomatoes and basil, 134
  ribollita, 66
  roasted Jerusalem artichokes
    with goat's cheese, roasted
    tomatoes and agresto, 147
  roasted vegetable salad with
    rocket and tomatoes, 76
  romesco, 148
  salt-baked wild salmon with
    roasted tomato aïoli, potatoes
    and purslane, 56–7

sauce vierge, 124
sea bass with mint, tomatoes
  and red onions, 133
slow-roasted tomatoes, 123
squash and tomato curry with
  lime and coconut, 130
tomato and apple ketchup,
  138
tomato and bread soup, 127
tomato sauce for pasta, 123
wild garlic and white bean curry,
  114
trifle: zuppa inglese, 244
turbot, 40, 42–3

vanilla ice cream with poached
  cherries and chocolate sauce,
  34
vinegar, 158–65
  bruschetta with aged balsamic
    vinegar, 161
  pan-fried mackerel with red
    wine vinegar, horseradish and
    crème fraîche, 164
  pickled cherries, 29
  pickled pumpkin with burrata,
    162
  slow-cooked shoulder of lamb
    with red wine vinegar, 165
  tomato and apple ketchup,
    138

walnuts, 140, 142, 143
  agresto, 147
  salad of roasted beetroot,
    walnuts, watercress and
    mascarpone, 144

watercress: pink grapefruit,
  avocado and watercress salad,
  74
salad of poached salmon, black
  rice and watercress, 82
salad of roasted beetroot,
  walnuts, watercress and
  mascarpone, 144
wild garlic, 168
  wild garlic and white bean curry,
    114
wild sea bass with salmoriglio, 68
wine: baked pears with honey,
  marsala and bay, 232
  baked Sauternes and honey
    custard, 231
  grilled rabbit with lentils cooked
    in red wine, 118
  mallard with porcini and red
    wine, 188
  roasted grouse with Barolo on
    toast, 192
  squid with peppers, red wine and
    wild marjoram, 58
  stracotto, 176
winter purslane see purslane

yoghurt: fried egg with sage, chilli
  and garlicky yoghurt, 170
  grilled poussins with lemon,
    marjoram, flat bread and
    garlicky yoghurt, 95

zuppa inglese, 244

Acknowledgements

Thank you first and foremost to my children, Holly and Evie, who let me go to work and do the thing that I love, even though I think they would prefer for me to stay at home.
A special thanks to all those I work with every day, for they make my working life such a joy.
Thank you to Jason Lowe for his beautiful photographs. It is always a joy to work with him, as it is to work with my editor, Janet Illsley, and designer Lawrence Morton. Thank you also to publishing director Jane O'Shea, and to everyone at Quadrille Publishing.

First published in 2008 by
Quadrille Publishing Limited
Alhambra House
27-31 Charing Cross Road
London WC2H 0LS
www.quadrille.co.uk

This paperback edition
published in 2009

Cataloguing in Publication
Data: a catalogue record for
this book is available from the
British Library.

ISBN: 978 184400 822 3

Printed in China

Publishing director
Jane O'Shea

Creative director
Helen Lewis

Project editor
Janet Illsley

Art direction & design
Lawrence Morton

Photographer
Jason Lowe

Stylist
Cynthia Inions

Production director
Vincent Smith

Production controller
Marina Asenjo